| DATE DUE | | | |
|---|---|---|---|
| AUG 1 1979 | | | |
| NOV 17 1980 | | | |
| DUE MAY 15 1991 | | | |
| DUE JUL 8 1991 | | | |
| | | | |
| NOV 23 1991 | | | |
| | | | |
| | | | |
| | | | |
| | | | |

Alternative Goals in Religion

*George Bosworth Burch*

With a Foreword by
*W. Norris Clarke,* S. J.

# ALTERNATIVE GOALS IN RELIGION

Love

Freedom

Truth

McGill–Queen's University Press *Montreal and London* 1972

Three of the poems which appear on pp. 76-77, "A strange old man" by Kakinomoto No Hitomaro, "When I went out in" by the Emperor Koko, and "No one spoke" by Ryota, are from Kenneth Rexroth, *One Hundred Poems from the Japanese.* All Rights Reserved. Reprinted by permission of New Directions Publishing Corporation.

This book has been published with the help of a grant from the Humanities Research Council, using funds provided by the Canada Council.

©McGill—Queen's University Press 1972
ISBN    0-7735-0122-3 (Cloth)
ISBN    0-7735-0163-0 (Paper)
Library of Congress Catalog Card Number 72-82248
Legal Deposit 4th quarter 1972

BL
51
B84

Design/Peter Maher
Printed in the U.S.A. by LithoCrafters Inc.

**51125**

To the Memory of
Srimant Pratap Seth
Founder of the Indian Institute of Philosophy
Industrialist, Philanthropist, Philosopher
Patron of Philosophers

# Contents

# Preface

WHEN I TOLD SRIMANT Pratap Seth, whose hospitality had encouraged and facilitated my first studies of Indian philosophy, that I wished to dedicate to him a proposed work on the philosophy of religion, I did not foresee that the writing would be so long delayed that he would not live to see the book. His long and fruitful life has ended, but his influence continues. I am indebted to Nancy Britton, Rasvihary Das, G. R. Malkani, Meredith Blodgett Poppele, and Beverly White (author of the goldfish haiku) for permission to use the passages quoted from their works. I am especially indebted to Professor W. Norris Clarke, S.J., for his critical foreword, in which the opposed view is presented with at least equal force, and by which the value of the book is greatly enhanced.

George Bosworth Burch
*Fletcher Professor of Philosophy, Emeritus*
*Tufts University*

# Foreword

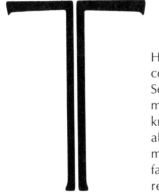HE AUTHOR, MY LONG-TERM colleague in the Metaphysical Society of America, has asked me to write this Foreword, knowing full well that I will almost certainly disagree with much of what follows. This very fact is a testimony to the truly remarkable breadth of spirit characteristic of Professor Burch. And even though I will in fact end up by disagreeing with him, this by no means diminishes my conviction that it is a profound and enriching intellectual and spiritual experience to meet the challenge he proposes.

The thesis proposed by the book is a truly radical one, so radical, in fact, that one experiences a kind of intellectual vertigo as he slowly awakens to what the author is really saying. The thesis, put simply, proposes a conception of the Absolute, as the goal of the great world religions, in which the Absolute is not one but many, that is, three alternative Absolutes, each equally ultimate and absolute, yet radically irreducible to each other or to any higher, more inclusive unity. It is a theory of the coexistence of three alternative Absolutes, which he describes roughly as: (1) Absolute Truth (or the Absolute Self as ultimate reality), corresponding to the religion of Hindu Advaita Vedanta; (2) Absolute Freedom, corresponding to Buddhism; and (3) Absolute Feeling or Love, corresponding to Christianity. The religious person must make an absolute commitment to one or the other of these Absolutes, such that he himself excludes the others for himself, while at the same time allowing full rights of coexistence to the others, on both the theoretical and the practical level, as objects of commitment and ultimate goals for other persons. An analogous model is that of monogamous marriage, where I can commit myself meaningfully and totally to this person or that, but not to both. As he puts it in the wonderfully pithy, down-to-earth way for which his writing, even on the deepest subjects, is well known: "From the fact that three girls are willing to marry me it does not follow that I can marry all three."

This theory of alternative and irreducible Absolutes is, so far as I am aware, quite a new one, both in the West and the East. Traditional theories of the Absolute, of no matter what vintage, have always held that the Absolute is one, although they disagree on how best to conceive it. To the challenge of coping with different conceptions of the Absolute in different religions and philosophical systems, the main traditional responses have been, as the author crisply sums them up: (1) dogmatism or dogmatic orthodoxy—this one is right and *not* that one; (2) toleration—this one *and* that one are both right, two different but equally valid ways of expressing and attaining the same one goal; (3) liberalism—neither this one nor that one is right in its exclusiveness of the other; the truth is a distillation of the common denominator shared by both.

Professor Burch's conception is quite different: all are equally right and valid, but only disjunctively, *either* A *or* B *or* C, and each person must make a total commitment to only one alternative (at least at any one time, though, of course, conversion is possible). For him, it is not a question of different paths to the same goal. Rather all the great religions start from roughly the same starting point, the condition of ignorance, suffering, and sin that is our present state, and then take divergent paths to divergent goals, or modes of liberation or salvation from this "fallen" state. For the Absolute itself exists in three alternative but ultimate and irreducible modes, with no reduction to a higher unity possible. This intellectual and psychological attitude of accepting coexistence between different irreducible commitments and their goals, together with mutual respect for each other, is the new mode of consciousness demanded for living together in a pluralistic world, which the author hopes will extend from the domains where it is already practised, that of monogamous marriage and the university world of irreducible but mutually respecting intellectual disciplines, to the wider and more socially crucial realms of international politics and world religions.

The inspiration for this truly radical conception of the Absolute probably came to the author from his study in India of the theory of alternative Absolutes proposed by the contemporary Indian thinker, K. C. Bhattacharyya, a theory which Professor Burch expounded brilliantly in an article entitled, "Search for the Absolute in Neo-Vedanta: The Philosophy of K. C. Bhattacharyya," in the *International Philosophical Quarterly* (December, 1967). As Editor, I immediately recognized the interest and significance of the article — actually a small monograph of 57 pages — even though its contents seemed to me so mind-boggling that I had a headache for three days after first reading it. Professor Burch has now apparently taken this theory for his own, adapting it in his own original way to our own contemporary scene.

Such is the kernel of the thesis propounded by the deeply challenging little book that the reader now has before him. I must now in all honesty give my own reactions to this theory, as the author has expressly invited me to do. It seems to me that there are two ways of understanding the Absolutes he is talking about. According to one of them I can agree with him, albeit reluctantly. According to the other—and I fear his more authentic and daring intention—I cannot, for the reason that it so shatters my own canons of intelligibility that I simply cannot see any way of affirming it without running afoul of contradiction. This, of course, does not prove it is not true in some domain unreachable by my logic, but only that I cannot see any way of affirming it as intelligible, not because I see it as mystery but as contrary to intelligibility.

On the first interpretation, the Absolutes in question are to be understood as psychological absolutes, that is, ultimate states of our own consciousness through which we become united with, or liberated into, the Absolute (about which in itself nothing at all can be said), or else, more objectively, aspects or facets of the one ontological Absolute, according to which our limited consciousness is united with the Absolute, each aspect being ultimate in itself and not explicitly revealing the others to our vision, but joined in a common root beyond any one angle of vision, even radically inaccessible to it. My ultimate mode of union with the Absolute would be according either to the mode of Absolute Truth (or as pure ultimate Self), or Absolute pure Freedom, or Absolute pure Love. Each of these would be an ultimate and irreducible mode of attaining the Absolute for a given human consciousness, and it is impossible to follow more than one way at a time. Thus there would be three ultimate and irreducible modes of experience and affirmation of the Absolute. Neither Professor Burch nor his Indian source of inspiration use the kind of language I have used above. But in an Indian thinker, where spiritual experience traditionally has the priority over abstract metaphysics (so much so that many apparently metaphysical theories are really only an abstract expression of spiritual experience and can only be properly understood if retranslated as an expression of this spiritual experience), such an apparent metaphysical theory as that of alternative Absolutes might well be only the objective expression of three ultimate and irreducible modes of spiritual experience.

Now adopting for the moment this understanding of the notion of alternative Absolutes, I am willing to admit, under the pressure of Professor Burch's challenge (although it does go against the grain of my more optimistic hopes for a future rapprochement of religions and mutual enrichment of religious experience through cross-fertilization of different religious traditions), that what he proposes may well be the case for us human beings, at least in our present lives or present mode of human consciousness. There might well be a radical, irreducible diversity of ways to attain the Absolute, which would demand a permanent pluralism of religions unable to be overcome by any effort of our present mode of religious consciousness.

Yet, while admitting this state of affairs as possibly the real one, and also that at present it does seem to be a stubborn fact that the paths of the great world religions do end up in a diversity of modes of consciousness of the Absolute which we can find no way to reduce to each other or transcend in some single higher unifying mode without doing violence to the authentic experience of each—while admitting all this, I say, I cannot but hope and long that this at present irreducible diversity may somehow someday be brought into greater unity by an interpenetration of these diverse modes, if only gradual or partial. And I certainly believe, on religious grounds of the unity of the spiritual history of mankind as children of one heavenly Father, that this will ultimately take place in some higher and definitive "next life" or "glorified life," as the Christians put it.

My reason is that I cannot bring myself to believe, with Professor Burch, that these modes of consciousness are in their ultimate purity unrelated and radically diverse from each other, as mutually exclusive alternatives. It seems to me rather, from the one concrete model of consciousness that we have available to our experience, that it is of the nature of consciousness to be radically one, and that these phenomenologically different expressions of it—truth, freedom, love—are all implicit dimensions of each other, though their interconnection at the root may remain in our present life only implicit and undeveloped, even beyond our present power to see how they can fuse into one.

Thus pure Truth, if it is to be a full and unqualified Absolute, and not an abstraction or limited focus of consciousness, must be inserted in and include the fullness of the real, and hence be conscious of the ultimate Self as pure freedom also and as such source of all else that is, insofar as this "all else" has some minimal degree of reality, even if only the reality of a dream. Pure Freedom of creative consciousness would also have to include, it would seem, the absolute Truth of its own reality as pure subjective Self, and whatever else it is the source of. And absolute Love would clearly seem to include both the luminousness of Truth and the pure creativity of Freedom. It is more difficult, I admit, to show how absolute Truth and Freedom necessarily include Love. This depends, perhaps, on how much one believes there is genuine duality in the real, though even without this, one could still speak of the bliss of self-embracing love. Thus each of these apparently exclusive Absolutes, if pushed all the way possible, would turn out to be implicitly complementary facets of the one absolute Consciousness.

Yet I am quite willing to concede to Professor Burch that it may be possible—and the actual fact—that different persons may concentrate so intensely on one or the other of these modes of consciousness that the others may recede into the shadow and appear to be simply absent. In other words, I believe an ecstasy of selective or limited consciousness is quite possible. These would be pure and in a sense ultimate states, but I would not personally like to call them "Absolutes," since they are not the ultimate fullness of consciousness possible in itself theoretically (perhaps even practically). Something would still remain undeveloped in them, shall we say in potency and not in full actuality?

Another reason why I am dubious about the possibility of multiple Absolutes, even as states of consciousness, at least if one understands "Absolute" as implying the total fullness of perfection possible, is this. To know *that* other ultimate positive states of consciousness are possible and exist for the choosing, and to know that one is not the other, is necessarily to affirm that each one lacks something that somehow is also real. *Omnis distinctio est negatio*, implying a negation of something positive at least in one of the members distinguished. Hence knowing this, at least abstractly, I could, it seems to me, and personally I would proceed to yearn concretely for all the absolute fullness of all modes of consciousness fused into one, with no negations whatsoever. I would long to go further than Ramakrishna and embrace all the fullness of all religious experiences not successively but simultaneously. How could one forbid the longing for and even possibility of achievement of this total fullness in some future form of life? If not, then nothing short of this total possible fullness would qualify as the unqualified Absolute in every way, in the sense of infinite plenitude. And the latter does seem to me an indispensable element of any absolutely unqualified Absolute.

Now let me turn to the second possible interpretation of Professor Burch's alternative Absolutes. On this view, these would not be merely psychological absolutes, or ultimate modes of human consciousness, but ontological Absolutes, which are in themselves, independently of my grasp of them, or commitment to them. In a word, can there be multiple ontological Absolutes?

Here I must reluctantly part company more decisively, I fear, with Professor Burch, although the theory in itself is so novel and mind-boggling that I may well be guilty of the fallacy of misplaced logic in all that follows. But I cannot affirm further than I can see, and it is only by the dialectic of opposing views that we can hope to draw a little closer to the core of the luminous Mystery that is the authentic Absolute, the ultimately Real. It seems to me that the requirements for an ontological Absolute in itself (as distinguished from a given human experience or mystical intuition of it) are at least the following: (1) it must be an unqualified or infinite fullness of perfection, hence allow of no negations (exclusions) of anything positive (unless, of course, that positive itself contains some built-in negation or limitation), since every such negation would imply a lack of the positive thus negated; (2) it must be utterly self-sufficient for its own being; and (3) self-sufficient as the ground for all other being or reality, however tenuous the latter's mode of presence may be.

Let me briefly comment on number three first. This requirement derives from the Absolute's role as ultimate principle of intelligibility, condition of possibility, or Source of all other being. The very meaning of intelligibility seems to me to involve drawing together all that we know into a unity, at least a unity of relation. "He who does not understand things as unities," St. Thomas Aquinas says, "does not understand anything at all." To understand is to unify what we know, to see how it all fits together. If one denies this unification process as a necessary component of intelligibility, I have nothing more to say and can only appeal mutely to our common experience of the effort to understand. This thrust toward unification is the very mainspring of all arguments and explanations, and hence cannot be justified by anything beyond itself.

Now my first difficulty is this: how can the identical datum of the finite imperfect world, from which all paths to the Absolutes take their start, be totally explained by, and dependent on, three distinct and totally unrelated Absolutes? The notion of three totally independent ultimate grounds for the same non-ultimate and dependent cosmic reality remains radically opaque in intelligibility, if not contradictory, to me. Hence I conclude that what we really are dealing with is not three simultaneous coexisting Absolutes, all three of which I must affirm as pre-existing goals for me to choose between, but rather three different and irreducible explanations or conceptions of the Absolute, only one of which each religious person can commit himself to as true. Each one would therefore hold that the Absolute is and can be only one, but that there are radically irreducible options in how we conceive it. The latter position I am quite willing to admit as being the case, at least in our present state of human consciousness.

Let me now turn to the implications of the first two requirements of the Absolute, as applied to Professor Burch's three Absolutes considered now in themselves and not in relation to this phenomenal world. Can there be a plurality of ontological Absolutes in themselves, not merely a plurality of irreducible human conceptions of an Absolute which each conceiver affirms must be one and one only? He who holds the metaphysical — and in this case metareligious — theory of alternative Absolutes, must affirm as part of this meta- or pre-religious theory that all three Absolutes exist simultaneously in order for me to have the possibility of a choice in my commitment to one or the other. Otherwise my contingent free choice would actually constitute the Absolute chosen or bring it into being — in which case the latter could hardly be an ontological Absolute at all.

Now since these three Absolutes must be affirmed, at least in meta-theory, to coexist, and since they are not identical — note that it is Professor Burch himself who has introduced the logical terminology of a strong "or" — then each one implies a negation of identity with the other: A is not B. Now to affirm such mutual negation or real nonidentity necessarily implies as the ground of its intelligibility that either A or B lacks something positive which the other has. *Omnis negatio est determinatio (limitatio)* and unless it negates something positive it cannot produce a real distinction. Hence at least two of these three Absolutes would have to be in some way limited, not including the total plenitude of all perfection possible. Hence they would not qualify as Absolutes in the traditional unconditioned sense of the term; furthermore, according to the traditional metaphysics of the finite, whatever is by its nature limited requires some determining cause other than itself why it is thus limited to this particular mode of perfection and no other. Each limited "Absolute" could be considered an ultimate in its own line, say Freedom, but this would still not include the fullness of the other two simultaneously existing modes.

There is a further difficulty. For the Absolutes in the line of Truth and Love, at least, would have to know the existence of the other Absolutes, or else be radically deficient in their own order of knowledge and love, more so than we ourselves, who by hypothesis would know all three, at least to some degree. And once such a relation of knowledge and love is set up, we are forced to affirm the interrelation of the Absolutes to each other, and the question of the unifying ground of this interrelation inevitably comes up. For any A can know B only if A either gives being to B or receives its knowledge from B by B's action on it. In either case, one of the two must be dependent on the other, and hence cannot be Absolute because it is not self-sufficient.

Professor Burch, however, may well object that the above logical "victory" is too easily won, won at the expense of transposing his "A or B or C" into "A and B and C" in the metalanguage. Then of course it doesn't work. Multiple coexisting Absolutes would indeed be unintelligible. But I reply that the logical relation "A or B" cannot be projected into the real or ontological order except in terms of something outside of either which functions as decision-maker or chooser. Thus it would be my contingent choice of commitment which would determine the actual existence of Absolute A and not of B. They could then hardly be ontological Absolutes in themselves. The only Absolute I can determine by my own choice is either a conception of the Absolute or a path to it, or both. And even then, if one person commited himself to A and another to B, I would have to affirm, it would seem, on the metalanguage level, that *both* A and B are valid, though not for the same person. Then this would imply, from the metalanguage point of view, that the non-identity of the two conceptions involves some principle of limitation — hence imperfection — on the part of the conceivers, though this may indeed be impossible to overcome at this stage of our human consciousness.

It may perhaps be objected that all the above logical reasoning falls short of the mark, since one has no right to apply ordinary logical rules to the Absolute at all. To this I can only reply that in this case neither can one apply the logic of either-or, as Professor Burch does, and then one could not even state the theory of alternative Absolutes. One could merely affirm the Absolute, or an Absolute Dimension of reality, with no further determination as to whether it is one or many. But even then one would be barred from making any negations, hence distinctions, within it, under pain of importing limitation, as I have shown. Now not to be able to make any distinctions within something is implicitly to affirm it as one. For that something positive is one needs no extra reason or explanation (to be is to be one); but that it is multiple does.

From all this I conclude that, at least according to the only logic and metaphysics I can make sense of, Professor Burch's alternative Absolutes cannot be ontological Absolutes existing independently in themselves prior to the religious person's commitment to one or the other of them; for in this case they would have to be affirmed in the metareligious or metaphysical language as simultaneously coexisting, hence "A *and* B *and* C." And this would imply mutual relation, at least of knowledge and of negation of identity, which would in turn imply limitation or lack of something positive in all but one of them. All of this implies that only one of them could be an unqualified Absolute.

The only viable status, therefore, that I can see for these alternative Absolutes is that they are pure ultimate modes of consciousness according to which I become united with, or simply become, some real facet or dimension of the total transcendent fullness of the Absolute in itself.

These are the Absolute *for me*, according to three ultimate and irreducible modes of conscious participation by me, only one of which I can participate in at one time, at least in terms of our present mode of consciousness in this life. This position I am willing to accept, under the pressure of Professor Burch's persuasive presentation, as one impressive, intelligible, and illuminating theory — corresponding also perhaps to the actual fact — of man's religious capacity at present, although I also cannot but hope that some day, somehow, at least in "another life," we may be able to overcome this selective, hence limited, receptivity to the Absolute in its total undimmed splendour.

But for the present at least I am willing to admit, with Professor Burch — and this I consider one of the most valuable contributions of the book — that we must allow the possibility of basic incommensurable dimensions of spiritual experience of the Absolute, irreducible to each other, exemplified in the great world religions. This involves a profound respect for each in its own originality and integrity, the disposition to let each one be its own self fully, and not to try and force from without any artificial reduction of one to the other on theoretical grounds, unless it also springs from the depths of free immanent spiritual experience itself.

Thus, after satisfying my metaphysician's conscience by emptying my quiver of all its theoretical objections, I am left free to agree most warmly in the practical order with the spirit of profoundly respectful coexistence he advocates between devotees of the world religions. Yet this disposition need not, it seems to me, prevent a totally committed follower of one religious Absolute from believing according to his option, or making his option because he believes, that his own version of the Absolute in principle somehow includes within it all that is truly positive in the others, though he cannot see exactly how, or at least cannot communicate this to his fellow travellers along other religious paths.

And yet, after all my efforts to throw the net of my concepts and logic around Professor Burch's truly "wild" theory of alternative irreducible Absolutes and domesticate it to something more easy to live with both theoretically and practically, I must still, in all honesty and humility, confess to a certain uneasy feeling that it may still stand beyond as a yet unscaled peak, accessible only to some completely different mode of thought I am unable to share. The only thing left is to invite each reader to make for himself the deeply purifying and enriching effort to come to grips himself with the author's profound and — in the West — quite original challenge.

W. NORRIS CLARKE, S.J.
*Professor of Philosophy*

*Fordham University*

# *One*   Not, And, and Or

RTHODOXY AND LIBERALISM
are basic religious concerns.
Who does not will to hold
right opinion, that is, to be
orthodox? Who does not will
to enjoy freedom, that is, to
be liberal? Nobody chooses
to be either heterodox or il-
liberal. Yet orthodoxy and
liberalism are irreconcilable. You cannot both stick to the
straight path and gather the daisies in the field. It does no
good to argue that your choice really includes the values
of the other choice. The orthodox may cry out,

> *Take me to you, imprison me, for I,*
> *Except you enthral me, never shall be free;*
> *Nor ever chaste, except you ravish me.*

But the liberal is not impressed. He does not choose to be
imprisoned, enthralled, or ravished, even by God. The
liberal may explain, "The wind bloweth where it listeth. . . .
So is every one that is born of the Spirit." But the orthodox
is not impressed. He listeth to have the Spirit lead him,
not blow him.

The orthodox has logic on his side. If you want to be good, you have to do what is right; if you want to produce beauty, you have to follow the canons of aesthetics; if you want to know truth, you have to think correctly. The impregnable fortress of orthodoxy is the law of non-contradiction. With two mutually contradictory doctrines, it may be difficult to establish that one of them is true, but once you have established it you do not have to be concerned with the other any longer. That is why the orthodox man pities the infidel but gets furious at the heretic. An infidel is one who does not accept your premises. A heretic is one who accepts your premises but rejects your conclusions; in short, he is not logical. You cannot, of course, argue with a person who rejects your premises, but you can exhort him to open his eyes to their truth. But there is nothing you can do with a person who won't be logical except burn him at the stake.

The formula of orthodoxy is *this not that*. This is true, ergo that is false if that is opposed to this. There is a right ism and a wrong ism — maybe several wrong isms but only one right ism. When I took "Contemporary Philosophical Tendencies" in college, realism was proved and naturalism, pragmatism, and idealism disproved, though when another professor gave the course it was idealism which was proved. This was in the spirit of orthodoxy. Orthodoxy does not mean intolerance. Tolerance, permitting others to express their views as a matter of civil rights without entertaining the possibility that they might be correct, far from being inconsistent with orthodoxy, presupposes it. But orthodoxy is opposed to liberalism. Christians, especially those of the Western Church, have always had a passion for orthodoxy, hence their obsession with creeds. It is said that, when the Romans conquered Greece, the Roman proconsul, bothered by the disputes of the Greek philosophical schools, proposed that all the philosophers meet together at Corinth, debate the issues, and decide which were the correct views, which he would then promulgate, so making further controversy unnecessary. A friend told me how a gentleman he met in Europe defined the doctrine of Christianity with unusual detail and precision. "This," he concluded, "is the Catholic faith, and those who believe this constitute the Holy Catholic Church; at the present moment I happen to be the only member." Both these stories illustrate the spirit of orthodoxy or dogmatism.

The liberal, on the other hand, is illogical. Not that he rejects reason as such. To "believe because it is absurd" is if anything super-orthodox, the extreme opposite of liberal. But the liberal has his own brand of logic. He repudiates the old-fashioned logic of two values, true and false. His prophet is not Aristotle but Hegel. Aristotelian logic was all right for the Middle Ages, but we have a new logic now, based not on the law of non-contradiction but on the law of dialectic. If a thesis is true, its antithesis is true also, and both can be resolved in a synthesis on a higher level of thought. Realism and idealism are both true. A war is settled not by fighting it out but by making an alliance between the opponents. Love is the rule, not hate. Love your enemies, even your ideological enemies. The business of thought is not to determine which of two antitheses is true but to find the synthesis which includes both. You do not have to sacrifice either antithesis, as the Aristotelian does. You keep both. The only thing you have to sacrifice is the law of non-contradiction. This, unfortunately, is just what old-fashioned people hate to give up.

The formula of liberalism is *this and that*. I am right but you are right also, even if we disagree. There are many paths leading to the same goal. Truth is one, but men call it by different names. If you go your way and I go mine, we shall come together in due time as our paths converge in one. Logically this convergence is synthesis, the synthesis which justifies the conjunction of two ways instead of insistence on one and negation of the other. This is the liberal's goal. He will be a Catholic in Spain and a Buddhist in Burma, but at home, which is probably Boston, he just holds to religion in general. His philosophy is pure love of wisdom transcending both realism and ideal-ism, and his God is the Absolute Idea in which all relative ideas are synthesized. Since all roads lead to the Absolute, there are no dead ends. We are free to think as we please, and freedom of thought is man's greatest glory, coordinate with his freedom of action. This liberalism has a powerful attraction for the magnanimous man, who condemns the orthodox as narrow-minded. It is in especially high repute in my own community, and there may be some geograph-ical basis for this. The streets of Boston are notoriously labyrinthine. You often come to a corner where you do not know which way to turn, but usually it does not make any difference, as one way will get you to your destination about as well as the other. As you approach Boston from Wellesley there used to be a fork with a sign which read, "Boston either way." That is liberalism.

Both orthodoxy and liberalism have difficulties. When the liberal accuses the orthodox of being narrow-minded, he is quite right. It is unabashed provincialism to assert that our way is the only way or even that it is the best way. We know that there are other churches, other faiths, other philosophies besides our own. It is hard for an edu-cated person to be orthodox. Neither in religion nor in other subjects can we easily maintain that there is just one way. We know too much.

But liberalism has its difficulties also. If an educated person knows too much to be orthodox, he thinks too much to be liberal. His interests are broad, but his logic is narrow, and when he accepts a premise he accepts its consequences also. He does not accept inconsistent state-ments, and a statement which is not true he rejects as false. An irrational liberal simply accepts inconsistent views simultaneously, ignoring logic. A pseudo-liberal, who accepts various views by showing that really, when properly understood, they can be reduced to his own view, is simply a dogmatist in disguise. But a true liberal abstracts the common part of opposing views, considers this their essence, and ignores their differences as superficial. This presumed Hegelian synthesis on a higher level is all too often, especially in religion, on a lower level. It is possible to be both a Christian and a Buddhist simultaneously, but you have to sacrifice two things — the essence of Christianity and the essence of Buddhism. I recall a conference of Catholics, Protestants, and Jews on the Judeo-Christian heritage in higher education. It was a very pleasant occasion, full of friendship, good will, and liberalism, but nobody really had much to say. What was there to say? We could agree on prophecies, but not their fulfillment; on the Old Testament, but not its meaning; on Abraham, but not his children. That is the difficulty with liberalism. Bahaism is a most liberal religion. The Bahais, in my experience, are very fine people, but it is not much of a religion. Theosophy, going to the other extreme, endeavours to embrace all religions, philosophies, and sciences in all their concrete richness. But such omniscience, perhaps possible for God, is hard for the rational but finite human mind, which combines differences only by transcending inconsistencies. Hegel's dialectic is a noble experiment in omniscience. The Absolute Idea has the merit of synthesizing everything but the demerit of being empty. And at its worst, liberalism degenerates into unctuousness; an illustration is this sentence from a recent article on Schubert, "Such thoughts centre not on the narrow sectarian ideas relating to the god of any one religion, but to that Supreme Power which, having brought the universe into being, orders its majestic harmony and beautifies its appearance."

The issue between the *notters* and the *anders* cannot be solved logically, because it is not a logical problem. It is a metalogical problem. The question is, what sort of logic are we to recognize? If we accept traditional two-valued logic, the logic of truth and falsity, then our problem is to find the truth, and having found it to defend it as orthodoxy, the right belief. If we accept the logic of liberalism, our problem is to synthesize opposed ideas as best we can. Neither way can acknowledge the other, and there is no super-logic by which to judge between them. But neither is fully satisfactory. The logic of orthodoxy fails to recognize the equal claim of the alternative, while the logic of liberalism is either irrational in uniting incompatible ideas or inadequate in ignoring much of their content. If we ask the metalogical question whether there is a third sort of logic besides these two, one such logic immediately suggests itself. Besides negation and conjunction there is also disjunction. Besides *not* and *and* there is *or*. I mean *or* in the exclusive sense: *this or that but not both*. "Boston either way" is liberalism. If the sign read, "Left Boston, right dead end," that would be orthodoxy. But who says we must go to Boston? Suppose the sign read, "Left Boston, right New York"? Who is to say that Boston is better than New York? With this sign we have a choice, but it is necessary to make a commitment.

*This or that* is the formula of commitment. A choice is offered but commitment is required. When the menu offers steak, chicken, or lobster, we do not insist that only one is edible. Neither do we order a little of each. We make an arbitrary choice and having made it are committed to it. Life is like that. We do not have a little of various vocations, various wives, or various religions. Yet it is only in retrospect that this vocation, this wife, or this religion seems the only possible one. At the time of choosing there was a real choice. But if we live in accordance with our commitments, we ourselves are formed by them. The other choices were possible for us as we were then, but they are impossible for us as we are now. We do not determine our commitments, for these are free, and a choice with no alternative is not commitment but necessity. Rather, we are determined by our commitments, which make us what we are. We can judge how well we have abided by our commitments, but we cannot judge the commitments themselves. How can I say that I am better than my friends who chose other vocations, wives, or faiths? How can I even say that I am better than I would have been had I chosen differently? I cannot compare the students I have with the nonexistent hypothetical patients I might have if I had chosen to be a doctor. I cannot compare the children I do have with the nonexistent ones I would have if I had married someone else. I cannot compare the religious experiences I have as an Episcopalian with the presumably different ones I might expect had I become a Quaker instead. Commitment involves the opposition of incomparable alternatives.

The logic of disjunction is the logic of faith, which requires indemonstrable and therefore arbitrary choice. If not the logic we think by, it is usually the logic we live by. It is a dynamic logic. The ordinary logic of *not* is static, merely making explicit the theorems already implicit in the premises. The Hegelian dialectic of *and* is only apparently dynamic, finding a more comprehensive formula for antithetical ideas. But the free choice of *or* involves progress, as one possibility is actualized. The alternatives are rejected, ignored, subordinated, or included, depending on their relation to the one chosen, and are no longer possibilities. The choice may generate new possibilities and so a continuing progress terminating only with the attainment of the Absolute. But this Absolute, unlike the inevitable Absolute of Hegelian dialectic, has alternatives.

The disjunctive attitude when applied leads to the policy of coexistence. In international relations this means that different countries may have different political systems, each wrong by the standards of the others but all equally good or rather incomparable. In social relations it means that different individuals may have freely chosen occupations and ways of life, unlike the predetermined vocations of a caste society or the unspecialized activities in primitive society. In philosophy, which is the speculative search for the Absolute, and religion, which is the practical escape from our non-absolute or sinful predicament, the disjunctive attitude offers an alternative to both orthodoxy and liberalism.

Philosophy, if it is to be existential and not mere analysis of concepts, must start from experience, whatever experience we actually have. Experience is complicated. It must be analysed and purified. Experience always includes consciousness and its content, that is, subject and object. But there are three ways in which they can be related. The content may determine the consciousness: this is *knowing*. The consciousness may determine its content: this is *willing*. Consciousness and content may mutually determine each other, producing values not reducible to either: this is *feeling*. In ordinary experience these three conscious functions seem inextricably confused. Our knowledge of truth is perverted by wishful thinking arising from the will, and emotional prejudices arising from the feeling. Our freedom of will is restricted by what we know and by what we feel. Our aesthetic enjoyment is corrupted by overemphasis on the object enjoyed or on the enjoying consciousness. The scientist who seeks truth must purge his knowledge of subjectivity, and the philosopher who seeks absolute Truth must purge his knowledge of all subjectivity. This is surely difficult but, at least some believe, not impossible. The goal is to apprehend objective reality in all the richness of its concrete being, free from the subjective limitations, prejudices, biases, categories of understanding, and forms of intuition which make it abstract, illusory, or phenomenal. This, if attained, is absolute Truth. Its attainment, or even the first step toward it, involves some sacrifice. You attain objectivity only by abandoning subjectivity. You get truth only by giving up freedom. If you are going to accept facts as a scientist does, you cannot impose your own fancies on the world as a poet does. The search for truth is an austere discipline. But who says I must search for truth? I may prefer to glory in the freedom of my will, in the God-like activity of freely creating. In that case I will follow the opposite procedure, purging my will of all objectivity, of all those non-subjective influences which keep it from being pure subjective freedom. This, if attained, is absolute Freedom. It means, of course, sacrificing that submission to object which constitutes truth. But who says I must seek either objectivity or subjectivity? I may prefer to combine object and consciousness in an emotional appreciation of aesthetic value. I can do this by following a third procedure, purging my feeling of separateness. Union of subject and object is love, and feeling freed from all separateness is absolute Love. But love requires sacrificing both freedom and truth, for in love, as in any feeling, consciousness neither completely determines nor is completely determined by its object, but is firmly united with it, each requiring the other. Feeling is the most primitive form of experience, before the distinction of subject and object makes possible the more abstract and sophisticated functions of knowing and willing; as Scheler says, man is an *ens amans* before he is an *ens cogitans* or an *ens volens*.[1] Love, consequently, may be considered a more primitive goal than either Truth or Freedom, but that does not necessarily make it either better or worse. In ordinary experience we have some truth, some freedom, and some love. But they result from incompatible functions of the mind, and the more we have of one the less we have of the others.

To attain absolute objectivity, that is, absolute Truth, is the goal of Vedanta. Moksha is pure truth purged of all subjectivism, that is, all error. To attain absolute subjectivity, that is, absolute Freedom, is the goal of Buddhism. Nirvana is pure freedom purged of all realism, that is, all constraint. To attain absolute togetherness, with God and each other, that is, absolute Love, is the goal of Christianity. Beatitude is pure love purged of all separation, that is, all sin. These statements, to be sure, are generalizations, for each religion has many sects with considerable differences. Christian Science is much like Vedanta, and Vaishnava Vedanta like Christianity, while Pure Land and Madhyamika Buddhism have similarities with Christianity and Vedanta. But the generalizations hold in general. In each case the goal is the Absolute. But the three forms of the Absolute are not identical. On the contrary, they are opposite extremes. The ways leading to them follow op-

1. M. Scheler, *Schriften aus dem Nachlass*. I. Zur Ethik und Erkenntnislehre, 2nd ed. (Bern: Francke Verlag, 1957), 356.

posite directions. The paths do not converge. They diverge. They are not three paths leading up to the same
mountain peak. They are three paths leading up to different mountain peaks, and you cannot get from one peak
to another except by making a fresh start at the bottom (as
the young poet Plato made a fresh start by burning his
poems when Socrates converted him to the search for
Truth). The paths have the same starting point, the valley
of ignorance, suffering, and sin in which we find ourselves, but they proceed in opposite directions. There is
no necessity to follow one rather than another, but only
one can be followed. They proceed divergently not con-
vergently, disjunctively not conjunctively, alternatively
not jointly. It is this *or* that. The forms of the Absolute to
which these paths lead are equally absolute. They cannot
be evaluated by each other or by anything higher. They
are alternative Absolutes.

The attitude of commitment, requiring an adventure of
faith, appeals to those who dislike the dogmatism of orthodoxy or the shallowness of liberalism. But it cannot be
defended by rational argument. One can argue only when
a certain sort of logic is presupposed. One cannot argue
logically about what logic to accept. If I prefer the logic of
*or* to the logic of *not* and the logic of *and*, I cannot maintain that the others are wrong. That would be to presuppose the very logic of negation which is rejected. Neither
can I maintain that the others are also right. That would be
to presuppose the very logic of conjunction which is also
rejected. I cannot even maintain that the three logics are
alternatively acceptable so that you may choose any one
but not more than one. That would be to beg the question
by presupposing the conclusion. To try to be logical in
metalogic is just as futile as to try to be physical in metaphysics.

I am not suggesting that there are alternative truths, or
denying that there is an absolute Truth which can perhaps
be approached in different ways. I am suggesting that
there are alternative values, of which Truth is one. It fol-

lows that there are not merely different religions but different kinds of religion with different, opposed, and incomparable goals. A religious man can take, toward other religions, the attitude of orthodoxy or liberalism or commitment. Psychologically orthodoxy reflects pride in the exclusive superiority of one's own way. Liberalism reflects excessive humility prepared to eliminate from one's own way anything incompatible with others. Commitment reflects a true and robust humility which, while maintaining its own way without compromise or qualification, still recognizes the equal validity of other ways not as errors to be tolerated but as alternatives also freely chosen.

# *Two*  Sin, Suffering, and Ignorance

ELIGION, IF IT IS PRACTICAL AND not mere worship, is escapism, an attempt to change our condition, to escape from the sinful state in which we are. I use the word *sin* here in the wide sense of badness in general, including suffering and ignorance. Religion involves recognition that something is wrong with our actual condition, belief in a possible condition which would be better, and a method for actualizing this potency. There are different religions because different teachers have emphasized different imperfections in our actual condition, envisioned different better possibilities, and taught different techniques for attaining these goals. If you believe escape from sin is by the grace of God mediated through Christ, you are a Christian; if you believe it is by submission to the will of God as revealed by the Prophet, you are a Moslem; if you believe it is by the elimination of desire through your own free will, you are a Buddhist; if you believe it is by realizing the fact of your identity with Brahman, you are a Vedantist. But if you do not believe that you *are* in a state of sin, then you have no religion at all, and if it is true that you are not, you certainly have no need of any. The fact of original sin, that man is by nature bad, is the common presupposition of all religions.

I wish to consider five theses concerning sin. First, that the doctrine of original sin is a humbling doctrine which makes us realize how bad we naturally are. Second, that the nature of the state of sin can be known only by faith. Third, that sin can be understood only as separation from God. Fourth, that the prospect of eternal sin is terrifying. Fifth, that salvation from sin is possible by different ways leading to the same eternal goal. I propose to refute all of these theses.

It is often considered that the doctrine of original sin, if true, is too bad. This degrading theory of human nature seems misanthropic at worst, pessimistic at best. Those who believe it find it depressing. Those who do not believe it get indignant about it, and especially indignant when it is applied to some sweet and innocent, though unbaptized, babe sleeping peacefully in his crib. The researches of Freud suggest that the babe may not be quite so innocent as he looks, but that is another story which has little to do with the logical issue. I submit that the doctrine of original sin, far from being pessimistic, is of all doctrines the most optimistic and comforting, the only ground of hope and aspiration. I do not mean this in the sense of the theory of supralapsarianism, according to which the Fall was a put-up job arranged by the Lord in order that he might have the glory of redeeming us, like a lover who upsets the canoe in order to save his sweetheart's life. There is a certain consistency in this theory, but it has never appealed to me. The Fall of Man was certainly a regrettable event. The cartoonist's astronaut who intervened just in time to stop the Martian Eve from plucking her fatal apple did a commendable deed. But the Fall was regrettable, so to speak, only before the event. Once it has occurred, it is not regrettable to know that it occurred. When you wake up finding yourself on the floor, it is not degrading to be told that you have fallen out of bed. This means that you can get back into bed. The alternative would be that there is no bed and so you have to stay on the floor. To say you have fallen out of bed does not make the floor either harder or softer, does not say anything at all about the floor. To say that our present condition is a state of sin, that is, a fallen state, does not make that condition either better or worse, does not say anything at all about it which we do not already know. We know by experience how good we actually are. We know we are not so good as we would be if we were better nor so bad as we would be if we were worse. We can easily imagine a better world, free from hatred and wars, or a paradise like that described in the old Puritan hymn, "where every day is Sunday and sermons never cease." And we can easily imagine a worse world, with even more chaos and delinquency. Sin or no sin, actual life is just as it is, neither better nor worse. But the doctrine of original sin teaches us that this our actual state is a state of sin, that is, it is not our best possible state. There is a better state from which as a species we have fallen and to which as individuals we may return. In the classical parable of the prince brought up as a peasant, he does not find it degrading to discover that the peasant state is not his proper state. The doctrine of original sin means that we have potentialities which exceed our actualities. To deny sin is to deny this.

The refutation of the second thesis, that the nature of the state of sin can be known only by faith, follows from the foregoing considerations. The fact of sin can be known only by faith, but the nature of the state of sin can be known without faith, is indeed the only thing which can be known without faith. We know the nature of the state of sin, that is, our actual state, by experience. We need faith for two other things: first, to know that this state is not the best state of which we are capable, that is, the doctrine of sin; and second, to know that there is a way by which we can escape from it, that is, the doctrine of salvation. A man blind from birth must learn from somebody else that he is blind and that he is curable, but he does not have to be taught the nature of darkness.

To come to the third thesis, while it is true that sin can be understood as separation from God, it is false that it can be understood only in that way. This is indeed the Christian way of understanding sin. God is love, and being separated from God we hate instead of loving, will the evil instead of the good, are sinful instead of righteous. This is a true account of our actual state, but it is not a complete account. Buddhism emphasizes another aspect of our actual state, the fact of suffering. That all life is suffering is the first of the Four Noble Truths. Vedanta emphasizes still another aspect of our actual state, the fact of ignorance. It teaches that our supposed knowledge is ignorance, our supposed experience is illusion, our supposed world is unreal, and our supposed truth is error. Each of these is an abstract way of describing the same concrete situation. Christian, Buddhist, and Vedantist all agree that life is characterized by hate, suffering, and ignorance, but each emphasizes a different aspect. The motive for this abstraction is found in their respective doctrines of salvation. Christianity has a technique for overcoming hate, Buddhism a technique for overcoming suffering, and Vedanta a technique for overcoming ignorance. The particular way of salvation determines what aspect of our common experience is of religious significance and consequently how the state of sin can be most significantly understood. All are equally true, and apart from some particular theory of salvation are equally significant as descriptions of this life lived apart from God in darkness and pain.

The story is told of a Texas rancher who after a long and prosperous life finally came to his eternal reward, looked over the boundless vista, and said, "Well, Saint Peter, heaven looks to me just like Texas," whereupon the gatekeeper answered coldly, "I'm not Saint Peter, and you don't know where you are." This story suggests an important truth. That the prospect of eternal sin is terrifying, is a notion with which we have been indoctrinated by overen-thusiastic evangelists. Hell doubtless has its drawbacks. There will be weeping and gnashing of teeth, but no doubt there is in Texas also. If circumstances should re-quire me to live in Texas, I do not suppose that it would be intolerable. The prospect is not in any way terrifying, and I do not see why hell should be. When I asked my Philosophy in Literature class, which was reading Dante, to write on the topic, "Would you like to be in Paradise?" they agreed almost unanimously that they would not. They found little attractive in Dante's heaven — "too much whirling about," as one put it. On the whole they pre-ferred hell. Criminals, to be sure, are punished there, but that is justice. The good people seem to have very pleasant accommodations. They are, of course, deprived of the presence of God, just as we are on earth. Faithful Christians hope to go to heaven to enjoy his presence. But my students, lacking that faith, saw nothing wrong with hell, and I must agree that there is nothing wrong with it. It is not good, by an absolute standard, but it is no worse than life on earth. It is, I suppose, simply a continuation of life like that on earth — though without the fear of dying or the hope of salvation. It is eternal sin, an endless life of our ordinary experience with its familiar hatred, suffering, and ignorance. We need not fear hell. The promise of reli-gion is not that it will save us from some state worse than that to which we are accustomed, but that it will exalt us to a state better than that to which we are accustomed.

The last of the five theses, that salvation from sin is by different ways leading to the same eternal goal, is a ves-tige of dogmatic provincialism. We are all by nature pro-vincial. We assume that our way is the right way, that our guru is the only guru, that the book we have enjoyed is a must for everybody. Education is a widening of our hori-zons and a consequent overcoming of provincialism. But there is a tremendous resistance to education, as teachers know so well, and this is perhaps most true in the case of religion. Like a powerful telescope which reveals distant stars at the cost of restricting the field of vision, religion seems to reveal profound truths only by narrowing the field of our spiritual vision. When we hear of other religions, our first impulse is to deny their existence. Religion is Christianity, and so the heathen, not being Christian, obviously have no religion. When further knowledge makes this position untenable, we say that the heathen do indeed have their own religions, but that these religions are false — like the many false answers to an arithmetical sum which can have only one true solution. Still further appreciation of heathen religions leads to the position that they are good and true so far as they go, but our religion goes further and is in fact the very truth the others are groping for. The Jewish Law is fulfilled by Christ, the Greek worship of the Unknown God is consummated by Saint Paul's message, and the Hindu religions are steps in the right direction needing only to be crowned by the full Christian truth, as Farquar puts it in that excellent missionary treatise *The Crown of Hinduism*. Still deeper insight leads us to say that all the great religions, even including our own, are of equal value, being coordinate and equally valid ways leading to the same goal of eternal beatitude in union with God (*our* goal, of course), and in saying this we pride ourselves on our scholarship, tolerance, and liberalism. You follow Buddha and I'll follow Christ, see you in heaven. This broad-minded view recognizes that there are many ways, but it keeps the old dogmatic and provincial prejudice that there is only one goal. We must face the fact that divergent roads do not lead to the same destination. What the various religions have in common is not their goal but their starting point. All start from the same situation in which we all find ourselves, the common state of sin, suffering, and ignorance.

The Christian way of understanding this state is set forth concisely in the Thirty-Nine Articles: "The condition of Man after the fall of Adam is such, that he cannot turn and prepare himself, by his own natural strength and good works, to faith, and calling upon God. Wherefore we have no power to do good works pleasant and acceptable to God, without the grace of God by Christ preventing us, that we may have a good will, and working with us, when we have that good will." Human nature is corrupted by the Fall. Fallen into sin, that is, separated from God, the intellect, not enlightened by eternal Truth, holds false opinions, and the will, not guided by eternal Love, makes evil choices. All men, since they are what they are by participation in human nature, are corrupt originally in intellect and will. Like persons caught in quicksand, they cannot save themselves but can only be saved by someone standing on firm ground. Such salvation is available, Christians believe, by the grace of God acting through the chain of events beginning with the Incarnation. There is a difference of opinion as to whether divine grace is irresistible, that is, whether God throws us a rope or lassoes us. According to some theologians God saves us from sin as the mother monkey saves her baby monkeys from danger, scampering up a tree while they hold fast to her fur with all four hands. According to others he saves us as the mother cat saves her kittens, carrying them off with no cooperation from them. Be that as it may, both the Fall and the Incarnation are great mysteries, cutting across the logical structure of the universe created through the Logos. The Fall is radically inexplicable and contingent. Although that irrepressible rationalist Saint Anselm tried to show that the Incarnation was logically inevitable, most theologians consider it a free and contingent act of pure grace, and I remember seeing, in the Vienna collection which visited this country, a painting which showed the three persons of the Trinity sitting around a conference table discussing whether they should go through with the proposed Incarnation. In any case, the Fall is our fault and the Incarnation is God's grace. We all *deserve* to go to hell.

The Buddhist world view is set forth concisely at the beginning of the Sermon of Banaras, Buddha's first public teaching. "Birth is suffering. Old age is suffering. Sickness is suffering. Death is suffering. The presence of things we hate is suffering. The absence of those we love is suffering. Not to obtain what we desire is suffering. All life, in short, is suffering. This is the aryan truth concerning suffering." It may be objected that life is a mixture of suffering and happiness, that it includes both gall and honey. This argument does not impress Buddha. The sweetness of life is discussed in the parable of the well. A criminal pursued by police hides by descending into a dry well by a vine growing down it. He looks down and sees a viper at the bottom, and clings to the vine for safety. As his arms get tired he looks up and sees two mice, a white mouse and a black mouse, gnawing at the vine. Suddenly he notices, just above his face, a beehive from which a few drops of honey are falling, and forgetting his danger he tastes the honey with delight. We are all like that criminal. The police are the desires of the body. The viper is its inevitable decay. The vine is the continuity of life. The white and black mice are day and night, the inexorable flow of time. The drops of honey are the rare pleasures at which we snatch so greedily. But such pleasures cannot save us from suffering. Only some radical reorientation of life can save us from suffering, for life as we know it is essentially suffering. To know this, the first of the Four Noble Truths, is the beginning of wisdom. To know it requires no revelation or faith, but simply recognition of the facts of life. To deny it is to shut our eyes to the obvious.

The Vedanta doctrine concerning the world is set forth concisely by Gaudapada, the founder of the non-dualist school of Vedanta philosophy: "Like a dream, like a mirage, like fairyland, so is this world, as Vedantists see it." Some non-dualists, to be sure, find it less simple. The celebrated philosopher Shankara distinguished between phenomena and dreams. God has created the world, not in the Christian sense of making something real, but like a magician creating an illusion, and we see the illusion because it is objectively there, although we can, by clear thinking, avoid being deceived by it. Within the world illusion there are subordinate illusions still less real, purely subjective, like dreams within a dream. Followers of Gaudapada do not accept any such ontological hierarchy among nonentities. Dream, mirage, fairyland, phenomenal world of ordinary experience differ in their psychological cause but not in their intrinsic status as nonexistent. Be that as it may, all non-dualists agree that the world is unreal, its appearance an illusion, and our knowledge of it ignorance. Knowledge of the unreal, whether more unreal or less unreal, is error. Truth is knowledge of the real. We see a snake, and are frightened. Then we see that it is really a rope which looked like a snake, and are no longer frightened, not because we have escaped or because it has gone away but because the error has been corrected. The simile of the rope appearing as a snake is tediously repeated by all writers on Vedanta. Apparently it actually is possible to make this mistake. Nancy Britton tells this anecdote in *East of the Sun:*

> As Frank and a shipmate emerged from the gents' bath with towels over their arms, the eerie nightlight in the hall picked out a thick coil waiting motionless under a table. They moved fast: one stood guard while the other dashed for a broom and clouted the thing hard. Then they both giggled so wildly that I looked out of the bedroom window to see what was up, which was just as well as they might not have told me otherwise. The coil was a rope from the window shutters.[1]

According to Vedanta the world is like that snake. No broom can kill it, and no broom is needed to kill it, because there isn't any snake.

Christianity, Buddhism, and Vedanta, emphasizing the wickedness, suffering, and ignorance of this life respectively, do not deny the two other aspects but lay less stress on them. Christianity has relatively little concern about the suffering, which it sometimes tries to explain as

1. N. P. Britton, *East of the Sun* (Edinburgh: Blackwood, 1956), 29.

somehow having a sort of value in itself; and the conscious bliss of the heavenly future life is considered an extrinsic reward of merit rather than the essence of beatitude. And it has relatively little concern about the ignorance, since knowledge of Absolute Truth is thought of as impossible or at best only for mystics, and not a condition of sanctity, which indeed is best sought in the attitude of a little child. Buddhism has relatively little concern about wickedness, which is automatically compensated through the working of the law of karma. And it has little concern about ignorance, Buddha refusing even to discuss metaphysical problems on the ground that such knowledge is useless. Vedanta has relatively little concern about wickedness, since salvation is by knowledge alone, or about suffering, which it considers only illusory. Concretely, apart from any of these abstractions, our actual experience is a mixture of sin, suffering, and ignorance. Insofar as the subject is separated from the object of his experience, he opposes his interests to those of others, and this is the source of that selfishness, wickedness, and hatred which constitute sin in the narrow sense of that word. Insofar as the subject is thwarted by objective facts which he cannot control, suffering results. Insofar as the object appears distorted by subjective conditions of awareness, we are ignorant of the objective reality. Psychologically our experience is a confusion of subjective and objective factors, and this confusion produces sin, suffering, and ignorance.

Our escape from this situation is described by Plato in his allegory of the cave. Some later thinkers, not appreciating a good allegory when they hear one, have tried to improve on it. Not satisfied with getting up to the surface of the ground, where Plato's philosophers contemplated the sun and other realities, they want to climb a mountain. If it is good to go up, it must be still better to go still higher. Hence the common metaphor of many paths leading up to the same mountain peak. But we must be careful in using metaphors, which are rhetorical devices, not demonstrations of truth. To call the better the higher is only a spatial metaphor. There is no logical reason to call the better "higher" rather than "lower." The source of this universal metaphor is obscure. It may be derived from the primitive situation of single combat, at the conclusion of which the weaker and so presumably worse man is flat on the ground, while the stronger or better man is still upright and so literally higher. But in any case it is only a figure of speech, and we are not necessarily better off because we are higher up. Dante, to be sure, represented degrees of goodness, negative or positive, as directly proportional to altitude below or above sea level, but Dante was a poet whose medium of expression was figures of speech. To return to Plato, there is doubtless an advantage in getting up out of a cave, but it does not follow that there is a similar advantage in going up a mountain. On the contrary, climbing a mountain is much like going down into a cave. Mountain climbers and speleologists have much in common, laboriously seeking to reach the tops of mountains or bottoms of caves, but with similar attitudes and motives. I like to climb mountains, but this sport does not strike me as a pattern for spiritual progress. It is a sport to be pursued for fun, but religion is serious. The goal of mountain climbing is a cold, windy, and uncomfortable summit where one would not want to stay, but I hope my religious goal is just the opposite. After you have succeeded in reaching the summit, there is then nothing to do but go down again, but we hope our spiritual progress is a one-way passage to our eternal home. If we must speak of mountains, we may say that different paths lead to different peaks, but it would be a better metaphor to say that spiritual progress is going *down* a mountain. The summit is analogous to our starting point, its isolation an analogue of sin, its windiness an analogue of suffering, its remoteness from the life of the world an analogue of ignorance. When we go down, we come to the valley, which is our true home, with its wealth of goods and interests. But the paths going down diverge, leading to different valleys, and this metaphor has a moral. If there is anyone in whose company you wish to enjoy your eternal felicity, you should follow the same path.

Whatever metaphor we use, cave or mountain, the truth which the figure expresses is that this life is relatively bad. It is not bad by our own standards, for it is what we are accustomed to, but it is bad by comparison with some better life. It is bad, relatively, because of its poverty. This is a poor life. Our love is reduced almost to zero by our selfishness. Our happiness is reduced almost to zero by unlimited desires inevitably frustrated. Our knowledge of reality is reduced almost to zero (Kant says completely to zero) by our subjective forms of intuition and categories of understanding. The life to which we aspire is a rich life, like the rich and fertile land extending without end outside the cave or below the mountain. To attain heaven or nirvana or moksha does not mean giving up the good things of life. It means getting more goods. Our love of God is richer when we are no longer separated from him, and our love of neighbour is richer when we love all men in God. Our happiness is richer when our freedom is no longer restricted. Our knowledge of truth is richer when we know reality in the richness of its concrete being instead of in some abstract form of our own imposition. Each of these consummations is possible, so we are taught. Nevertheless, it does not follow that they are possible together. We must beware the fallacy of composition: because three girls are willing to marry you, it does not follow that you can marry all three. Absolute Love, Freedom, and Truth may be incompatible. In that case we may have to give up something after all. This is a question into which we must inquire.

But before leaving the subject of sin, suffering, and ignorance, we must remark on a paradox in the notion of salvation from any of them. A friend of mine, greeted at the door by an evangelist from one of the Holiness sects with the standard challenge, "Have you been saved?" answered, "Yes," and when the evangelist, a little taken back, inquired, "When?" replied, "On Good Friday, 33 A.D., at three P.M., Eastern European Time." No doubt he was saved then, but still—is he saved? Properly speaking he was redeemed, not saved, on that occasion. Redemption is *de jure* but not *de facto* salvation, analogous to a Supreme Court decision that segregation is unconstitutional, while salvation is analogous to the enforcement of this decision by actual desegregation, a very different thing. The citizen deprived of his rights gets only scant consolation from the knowledge that this is unconstitutional, and the sinner lacking grace gets scant consolation from the knowledge that Christ died for him. Christ by his sacrifice on the cross has redeemed mankind from sin— still we are all conceived in sin and must win our salvation individually, if at all, with the help of the third person of the Trinity. Buddha took a vow not to accept nirvana until all sentient beings were freed from suffering, and he has now entered nirvana, two and a half millennia ago, ergo all sentient beings are free from suffering—but sentient beings still suffer and must win their own nirvana individually if at all. The Self of Vedanta is the Absolute, and in realizing this it has brought ignorance to an end, awakening, as it were, from the dream which individuals are mere figments of—yet each individual is still subject to illusion and must attain enlightenment individually if at all. According to Augustine some are predestined to be saved, others not; according to Origen all will be saved sooner or later, one by one; according to Erigena it is Mankind, as such, which falls and which is saved. These three points of view—elective, universal, and collective salvation—are found in all three religions. But in all three the paradox remains: we are saved eternally, but we still have to be saved individually. Associated with this paradox is the question of the help to be given by the saved to those not yet saved. Plato taught the enlightened philosopher's obligation to go back down into the cave to assist those still in the bonds of ignorance (a categorical imperative not conditioned by any anticipation of success). But in religious teaching there has always been a difference of opinion concerning either the obligation or the possibility of such help.

Catholics expect the saints in heaven to perform miracles for the benefit of people still on earth; in fact, this is how the saints prove to us that they are in heaven. Protestants, on the other hand (following the example of Abraham, who flatly refused to send Lazarus from heaven to warn Dives's brothers of their danger), expect the saints to eschew any intervention in worldly affairs and do not invoke their help but pray only to God. Mahayana Buddhists give their highest reverence to the bodhisattvas who, themselves perfectly enlightened, through compassion sacrifice their own freedom in order to help others. Hinyana Buddhists, on the other hand, believe that each individual must save himself by following the Buddhist way of life, and that the person who has done so cannot help others because he ceases to exist. Anekajivavada Vedantists believe that the individual freed from illusion has, at least in his own lifetime, if not the duty at least the possibility of directing the spiritual progress of those not yet freed. Ekajivavada Vedantists, on the other hand, object that there are not any individuals freed from illusion, because individuality is the illusion from which we are freed. But whether with or without the grace of those who have arrived, the religious path is more difficult than the optimistic claims of the established religions would make it appear.

Sin, suffering, and ignorance are very persistent. For all the bodhisattvas who have freed us from pain, it still prevails, and despite the Self's recognition of its own unique reality, we are still deceived. But it is in the Christian tradition that this truth is spelled out most clearly. The bitter fact is that sin is very difficult to overcome. I do not mean difficult for us, but difficult for God. Let us look at the record. The Lord's original idea in creating was to make angels, and he did so. But the angels fell, at least many of them did, leaving those embarrassing vacancies in the celestial court. The Lord then made a fresh start, creating man on a somewhat different plan. But man fell also, and soon a race of wicked men were filling the world with iniquities. Unwilling to make a third try, since the six days allotted to creation were spent, the Lord resorted to eugenics, breeding the human race from the one righteous man he could find and ruthlessly drowning the rest. But this did not work either; Noah himself was a drunkard, and his descendants were soon as bad as their predecessors. Stopped by the covenant of the rainbow from holding a second purge, the Lord abandoned the project of having the whole human race righteous and decided to concentrate on a chosen people, leaving the rest to the Adversary. Abraham was chosen, his descendants were given a Law after a preliminary disciplinary period, and they were provided with a small but adequate territory, the Lord himself sending hornets to dispossess the previous inhabitants. The Old Testament tells the tragic story: soon the Jews were just as bad as the Canaanites, if not worse. As a last resort God sent his only begotten Son to be himself a sacrifice for our sins, and "He died to make us good." *A priori,* this could not fail; empirically, we need only look around us to see whether it did. We may have faith in the ultimate triumph of love, freedom, and truth, but so far the Devil seems to be ahead.

# *Three*   Christianity

HE NEXT THREE CHAPTERS are concerned with the way to Love, the way to Freedom, and the way to Truth. I do not say the way *of* love, *of* freedom, or *of* truth. Love, freedom, and truth are values and therefore goals, not ways. If completely purged of all qualifications which make them relative to something else, they are absolute values. But it does not follow that they are identical. The prejudice that the Absolute is one is a consequence of that unity-mongering which has always been the bane of philosophy. That these three absolutes are really one Absolute is not obvious or even plausible, since going in different directions is an unlikely way to arrive at the same destination. But if in practice the way determines the goal, so in theory the goal defines the way. The goals of Love, Freedom, and Truth define the ways of Christianity, Buddhism, and Vedanta, respectively.

Various Christian sects embrace various heresies, but there are two fundamental heresies which all Christians, or almost all, reject, atheism and pantheism. Atheism means that there is no God; pantheism, that there is nothing except God. Between these extremes Christianity follows the middle way of theism, which means that there is God and there is also that which is not God. Atheism and pantheism are not incompatible with religion. Buddhism is atheistic, and Vedanta can be called pantheistic in a wide sense of the word. But atheism and pantheism are incompatible with a religion of absolute Love. If there is not God, there is no absolute object of love. If there is nothing except God, there is nobody to love God. Saint Augustine, to be sure, maintained that the Father and the Son love each other eternally, independently of creation, but this has nothing to do with religion, which is salvation for man. Love is consensus of wills without confusion of substances. It requires two persons. And if duality is the presupposition of love, so is love the evidence of duality. By pure reason it is difficult to escape solipsism. We see this clearly in the thought of Descartes, one philosopher who took the problem of the existence of the external world seriously. He established his own existence cogently by the self-evident axiom *Cogito ergo sum*, but to prove rationally the existence of something beyond himself he resorted to a devious, protracted, and unconvincing argument. Emotion, however, cuts through the boundaries of reason. If reason asserts *Cogito ergo sum*, love asserts, with equal self-evidence, *Amo te ergo es*. Love is the evidence of another person's existence, which pure reason can never prove, and ultimately it is the evidence of God's existence. All the famous rational proofs of the existence of God have never yet convinced a person who did not already accept it on other grounds, but love needs no demonstration. Atheism may be the theology of freedom and pantheism the theology of truth, but theism is the theology of love.

When Christ declared, "Thou shalt love the Lord thy God with all thy heart, and with all thy soul, and with all thy mind, and thou shalt love thy neighbour as thyself— on these two commandments hang all the Law and the

Prophets," he was not prescribing some preliminary discipline but was indicating the essence of the Christian life. When Saint Paul spoke of faith, hope, and love, he added that "the greatest of these is love." When Saint John said, "God is love," he identified love with the Absolute. When Saint Augustine summarized Christian ethics in the formula, "Love, and do as you please," he taught that love supersedes all other principles. Christianity is the way to Love. But just what is love? That is what we must inquire into.

It is customary to distinguish between *eros* and *agape,* Platonic love and Christian charity. The Biblical passages just cited have the word *agape.* Conceptually *eros* and *agape* are quite different. *Eros* is attraction motivated by the goodness, beauty, or lovableness of the beloved object — an attraction which should evoke a response in any subject, since the nature of the subject is not involved. *Agape* is benevolence motivated by the loving nature of the lover — a benevolence which should extend to any object, since the nature of the object is not involved. God, who is absolute Goodness, as Plato taught, is the supreme object of love for all persons, indeed for all beings, and finite beings are proper objects of finite love insofar as, and to the extent that, they participate in goodness or beauty and so are lovable. On the other hand, God, who is absolute Love, as Saint John taught ("Being and Love," according to Pope Paul's recent creed), is the supreme lover who loves all things indiscriminately, because it is his nature to love, and individual men are indiscriminately benevolent insofar as, and to the extent that, they have, by grace, been infused with love and so become godlike; Saint Francis kissing intrinsically unattractive lepers is a classic example. It is sometimes said that rational philosophy teaches that we, and all creatures, should love God because he is good, but that it is the peculiar, revealed, and non-rational teaching of Christianity that God loves us even though we are not good, and that we should love our neighbours even though they are not good, even if they are our enemies. This is doubtless so, and the perfect Christian, like Saint Francis, does love indiscriminately. But perfect Christians are rare. As a matter of fact Christians have never gone in for *agape* very seriously, in spite of their professed commitment to it. Except for some saints like Francis, who loved animals, plants, and inanimate objects, Christian charity finds its widest expression in a pacifism which teaches love for all men. But Buddhism teaches "compassion for all sentient beings," with vegetarianism its practical expression. Christians who abstain from meat during lent do so ascetically, for the sake of their own spiritual welfare, not benevolently, through concern for the animals. Jainism goes beyond Buddhism to teach benevolence even for plants (an attitude expressed also in Schweitzer's "reverence for all life"), and Jains actually make a serious attempt to follow this ideal. The American existentialist Henry Bugbee in his book *The Inward Morning* goes still further to teach "respect for things," all things, because they exist — a true existentialism which cuts across the relative evaluations produced by our subjective categories of value to recognize the objective and absolute value of being itself.[1] Be this as it may, the fact remains that Christianity, even in its theory, to say nothing of its practice, teaches a very limited sort of charity. If *agape* is the essence of religion, Christianity is not one of the more advanced religions.

In thinking of Christian charity, perhaps we should take our cue from Saint Paul, so that, instead of thinking of charity as coordinate with or somehow opposed to love, we think of it as the third and greatest of the trio faith, hope, and charity. These three theological virtues presuppose an inequality among men. There is always somebody higher than ourselves (if I may use that spatial metaphor) and there is always somebody lower. Any man of faith looks up to his guru or teacher, whoever or whatever or

---

1. H. G. Bugbee, *The Inward Morning* (State College, Pa.: Bald Eagle Press, 1958), 155.

however manifold that guru may be, as somehow superior and so a source of enlightenment, and he looks up to those who are higher on the path. The layman looks up to the priest who preaches the word of God, the secular to the monk who follows the evangelical counsels of perfection, the ordinary Christian to the saints. The greatest saints and mystics look up to Jesus. And even Jesus frequently spoke of the Father to whom, ignorant as he was of the Athanasian Creed, he looked up.

Every man also has others who are in some way or other inferior to him — physically, intellectually, spiritually, or in situation — although an individual inferior in one way may be superior in another. Even the worst man in the world can look down on sub-human animals. Now faith is the Christian's attitude toward those above him, hope his attitude toward himself, and charity his attitude toward those below him. By faith we turn to persons we believe to be in some way superior, and therefore able to enlighten our intellect by truth we cannot know by ourselves or to inspire our will by motives not natural to us. By hope we aspire to become ourselves better than we now are in some respect or other. By charity we serve those who are in some way inferior, giving them money if we are richer, information if we are more learned, comfort if we are stronger, help of any sort if we are more fortunate in any way. Faith, hope, and charity are the ways of the Christian life. But love is its goal.

The main entrance of the Stanford University chapel is adorned by four allegorical figures labelled Love, Faith, Hope, and Charity. I assume that this ill-advised expansion of the theological virtues was motivated by the architectural requirements of a facade with four niches, not proposed by the department of religion. To distinguish *eros* from *agape* is sound, but it would have been better if they could have found a central or higher position for Love, which is not coordinate with the others. When Saint John wrote that God is *agape*, he was revealing a peculiar Christian dogma not known to the rationalist tradition, but he was not denying that God is also *eros,* the "Love that moves the sun and other stars," that is, the Good which is the Prime Mover of the world by its force of attraction. When Saint Paul praised faith, hope, and charity, he was teaching the Corinthians how to be Christians, but he was not denying that the love of God was the goal of their discipline. Saint Bernard, anticipating William James's theory of emotion, taught that active charity (*charitas actualis*) is a cause which produces emotional love (*charitas affectualis*). But love (*amor*), he also says, is an end in itself: "Its use is its fruit; I love because I love; I love in order to love."[2] Charity is service, and for God it is grace, but love is union. *Agape* presupposes inequality, but *eros* produces equality, and even the love of God generates an ineffable quasi-equality in which the metaphysical difference between creature and Creator is somehow lost in the psychological union of lover and Beloved.

If love is union, lack of love is lack of union or separation, and this is sin. I now use the word *sin* in its strict sense, distinguished from suffering or ignorance, not including them. We might make a distinction after the analogy of the legal concepts of petty treason and high treason. Petty sin is separation from anybody, and high sin is separation from God. Such separation is our natural state: that is the doctrine of original sin. The symptom of sin is malevolent behaviour. To hurt anyone is petty sin. To oppose goodness as such, as young (later Saint) Augustine did when he stole pears just *because* it was wrong, is high sin. The distinction has little practical significance, however. Like radii of a circle with God at its centre, we draw nearer to each other as we draw nearer to God. To love God while indifferent to neighbours may be possible for a hermit, and to love neighbours while indifferent to God may be possible for a humanist, but normally either of these situations, while logically conceivable, is psychologically difficult. What is significant is that love is not our

2. Bernard of Clairvaux, *Sermons on Canticles,* 50, 2; 83, 4.

natural state. Consequently it has to be acquired: that is the doctrine of grace. To understand the doctrine of grace does not require any profound study of dogmatic theology. It follows from the fact of original sin and the law of sufficient reason. We can be good only by goodness, and if we are not good naturally we can become good only if goodness, that is, God, comes to us. God may act on us directly in a religious experience, but usually God acts on us through some instrument, so that we become good, if at all, through the influence of some person or thing or combination of such in our environment. But the fact that an instrument intervenes between God and ourselves must not blind us to the fundamental fact of grace. From our own point of view we become psychologically loving, metaphysically good, or behaviouristically righteous through the influence of something acting on us, not by the unassisted growth of our original nature.

This is what we profess as Christians, but what we actually believe is just the opposite. Our beliefs have been influenced much more by Rousseau than by Calvin. Rousseau taught that man is by nature good but that there are forces working to make us bad. Calvin taught that man is by nature bad but that there are forces working to make us good. If in either case we resist these forces, or avoid them if they are irresistible, we shall stay good or bad respectively. Calvin's theory is the Christian one, but most professed Christians believe Rousseau's. This is especially clear in our attitude toward children. We consider the little baby to be innocent, and not without reason, since he does look innocent. We just do not believe that he is in a state of utter depravity rightly deserving eternal damnation. So long as he is not old enough to commit overt acts, either good or bad, we give him the benefit of the doubt. There is no harm in this; the difficulty begins when he is old enough to be manifestly naughty, cutting off the kitten's fur or hitting the baby next door with a stick or telling a lie. Calvinists take this in their stride, for it is just what they expect, but what consternation for the followers of Rousseau! The parents make a threefold response: they are astonished, they punish him, and they avoid blaming him. In the first place, they are astonished, father arriving home to be met by tearful mother sobbing out that Johnny told a lie and asking what they did wrong to turn their good baby into a bad boy. In the second place, they spank him, explaining that it hurts them more than him, which is probably true, since as Plato pointed out it is worse to injure than to be injured, although the trauma to the child may be considerable also. In the third place, they do not blame the child but blame themselves for bringing him up so badly or perhaps blame the pernicious influence of some playmate. When he is older and becomes a juvenile delinquent, they will blame society in general for providing such a bad environment. When he is an adult and murders someone, he will be acquitted on the ground of temporary insanity. We never blame the delinquent himself unless we are angry, and then our reaction is an emotional, not a rational, one. Consider how different is our response to intellectual delinquency. In the first place, we are not astonished when the child learning to write makes errors in spelling. No philological Rousseau has taught that children naturally spell correctly until corrupted by bad influence. We accept the fact that he has to learn to spell correctly, and that we have to teach him to do so, and we proceed to the task with great patience. In the second place, we do not punish the bad speller, but reward the good one. The winner of the spelling bee is rewarded at least with prestige, while the loser is consoled by starting at the top next time (though now spelling bees have been generally abolished on the ground, as I understand it, that the loser might have his sensibilities hurt). In the third place, we do, except in progressive schools, insist that the bad speller is wrong. There is a correct spelling and an incorrect spelling, and the one who follows the latter is wrong. He was in fact born that way, with no innate knowledge of spelling, in a state of utter orthographical depravity. It would be wiser to respond to moral delinquency in an analogous way, as we would if we took seriously the basic doctrines of Christianity. In the first place, we would not be astonished by the child's bad behaviour. That would not make the behaviour any better, but it would enable us to relax. It would also enable us to correct it if we realized that it is our duty, as the relevant channels of grace, to do something to make him better, not just refrain from doing something to make him worse. The answer to the parents' question, what did they do to make him so bad, is quite definite: they conceived him in sin. Their task now is to change him, to teach him to be good, by precept, example, and other suitable techniques. In the second place, we would reward rather than punish. Too often we hesitate to reward children for good behaviour lest we give them the impression that such good behaviour, since we notice it, must be unnatural. But it is unnatural if man is by nature bad, and should be noticed. I doubt that punishing children is ever desirable, but rewards are both right in principle and effective. We should reward our children for being good because we must teach them to be good, and we must teach them to be good because they are naturally bad. In the third place, we would blame them and hold them alone responsible for their own delinquency, avoiding the quibbles of the Defense Attorney's Fallacy, the argument that a bad person is not bad because there is a reason why he is bad. The Moslem judge answered the murderer who sought acquittal on the ground that the victim was eternally predestined to be slain by pointing out that the murderer was likewise predestined to be hanged for it, and the jurors can respond to the attorney's claim that his client could not help committing the crime, brought up as he was, by considering that they cannot help convicting him of it, brought up as they are. Persons behave badly because they are in fact miserable sinners, separated from God, and the evil is in themselves. We shall never correct evil unless we recognize it. We must teach our children to be loving, good, and righteous because they must learn it.

They must learn it, that is, if they are going to progress toward love. There is no logical necessity; we can let them grow up delinquent. But progress toward love requires an influence from without. That is what is called grace.

To say that by nature we do not have love and that by grace we may acquire it is still not to say what love is. Poets, psychologists, philosophers, theologians, and mystics have laboured to define love in their various ways. For the purpose of comparative religion we must consider it from the metaphysical point of view. Love, that is, the erotic, Platonic sort of love, not mere benevolence or charity, is emotion or feeling. Charity may be carried out austerely, as rationally acknowledged duty, because of an imperative either hypothetical or categorical, without any feeling, and often is, as when we send another five dollars to the fund without really wanting to. But love is never reluctant. Love is appreciation of beauty, and the meaning of love is found in the meaning of beauty. Beauty is something which is felt. A simple case is the appreciation of an observed work of art, for example, a symphony. According to some philosophers the beauty is in the observer's mind. Objectively the symphony is a mere scratching of sheep's intestines by horses' hairs. The resultant beauty is mental, a secondary quality, or as some say a tertiary quality even less objective than such secondary qualities as sounds or colours. This theory, I should suppose, can be held most easily by someone who is not actually experiencing the beauty in question. The person who is experiencing it does not find it in himself. Sounds and colours may be only in the mind, a theory with much to recommend it, but beauty involves feeling which transcends the subject and value which irradiates the object. According to other philosophers the beauty is in the beautiful object, independently of its being observed by anybody. The beauty is determined by the form, in the case of music by the rhythm, melody, and harmony. The problem remains, to be sure, why harmonious music should be more beautiful than discordant music (a principle questioned by some modern musicians). For Pythagoras harmony is beauty, but for Plato harmony only makes the music harmonious, and only beauty can make it beautiful. But insofar as the music does participate in beauty, it is beautiful, whether or not anyone appreciates or even hears it. This theory, I should suppose, can be held most easily by someone who has not actually composed music. The composer (if I may speak of matters I know only by hearsay) does not merely manipulate forms but hears the beauty, and that is how he knows what forms to manipulate. Neither the subjective nor the objective theory seems adequate. Neither a beauty which is in the mind nor a beauty which need not be experienced is the beauty which is felt. Feeling is a union of subject and object. In other conscious functions, knowing and willing, subject and object are sharply contrasted, one subordinated to the other. In feeling the attempt to contrast them results only in destroying the feeling. The objective form of the music may remain, and the subjective appreciation may remain, but their union is lost and with it the feeling. This is even more clearly true when appreciation of the beauty of a person is exalted to love. Love is sympathy, feeling with, neither objective nor subjective. To be lovely is not to be loved, and to be in a loving mood is not to love. The lovely object needs a lover, not as a foil for her beauty, but to actualize what is otherwise a mere potency. The loving subject needs a beloved, not as a stage for his conscious mood but to transcend it by transcending himself. Every sort of love, physical or spiritual, is essentially a union. Metaphysically, feeling is union of subject and object, that is, of consciousness and content.

Whether we call it feeling, appreciation, or love, we are usually loving persons and things more or less, and the more we love the more our behaviour is altruistic. The opposite of love is selfishness, which becomes hate when an unloved object opposes our own interests. Selfishness is not a kind of feeling but emotional indifference, just as ignorance is not a kind of knowing but cognitive indifference, and hatred is not a kind of knowing but cognitive indifference, and hatred is not a kind of feeling but positive lack of feeling, as error is positive lack of knowing. Love, in short, makes us good instead of sinful. But love involves sacrifice. Love, truth, and freedom are incompatible. The scientist devoted to truth, bound to accept the results of his observations and calculations, however unpalatable, sacrifices his freedom, and the fact that he does so gladly does not make him free. He is not for that reason inferior to the free poet, for there is no norm by which truth and freedom can be measured, but he is different. To say he is really free is the fallacy of definition by initial identification, in this case recognizing freedom as a value and then inferring that value must always involve it. The poet, conversely, sacrifices truth, and to say that he really sees a deeper truth is to misapprehend what poetry is. The poet is a maker (*poietes*), not a knower. To feel is to sacrifice both truth and freedom. On the one hand, just as there is no place for feeling in science, no place for music in musicology, so there is no place for science in feeling. To know a girl as she is is a project for an anthropologist, not for a lover, who neither knows nor cares to know her as she is in herself but knows her as she is in union with him. To know God as he is in himself is a project for a theologian, not for a mystic, who seeks to know God as the Bridegroom of the soul. Cherubim, we are told, have perfect knowledge of God and seraphim perfect love of God, but not even angelic spirits can have both. Truth is to apprehend something as it is objectively. Love is to apprehend something as merged with yourself. Knowing frees the object from its subjective conditions. Feeling binds the object to its subjective conditions. This is an existentialist doctrine based on analysis of experience, and it rejects the idealism of the poet Keats, who said beauty is truth, the rationalist Plato, who said dialectic and loving both apprehend the one Good, and the monist Plotinus, who said the love of beauty, the path of knowledge, and the prayers of the devout are three ways leading to the same goal of union with the One. On the other hand, to feel is also to sacrifice freedom. To be free is to act voluntarily, to impose your own will on the object of your action, and this is just what feeling does not do. In feeling the subject does not dominate the object but appreciates it. In love the lover does not rule the beloved but merges his will with hers. You can force your will on somebody weaker, but you cannot force your love. In feeling or love you must submit, not to the object, as in knowing, but to the togetherness, and so renounce freedom, although gladly. Donne's verse, "I, except you enthral me, never shall be free," is great poetry but not literally correct. Freedom defies God like Prometheus, declares him dead like Nietzsche, or ignores him like Buddha. The more love, the less truth and the less freedom — a welcome sacrifice, for a lover desires neither truth nor freedom. In ordinary experience aesthetic enjoyment and love are restricted by knowing, which lets the object dominate consciousness, and willing, which lets consciousness dominate object. We purify our feeling by giving up either of these forms of separation and attain pure feeling when all separateness is gone.

Mystical love differs from other love not in its nature, for it too is union of consciousness and content, not in its intensity, for a trivial or carnal love may be intense, but in its object. The mystic loves God, the absolute Being. There are many disciplines by which this love is fostered. The Benedictine Order, for example, is described in its Rule as a school of charity, where the curriculum proceeds from the fear of God, which is the beginning of wisdom, to the love of God, which is its end. In general we can distinguish three degrees in the love of God. The first degree is that faith, common to all Christians, by which God is recognized, although imperfectly, felt, although vaguely, and loved, although inadequately — a union of the soul with God, but not an absolute union. By faith, however imperfect, we come in contact with, and so to some extent feel and love, the absolute Being, and thus are lifted to a higher level of feeling than any love of finite objects can involve. The second degree is mystical ecstasy, in which, to quote Saint Bernard, the soul may receive God "in the inmost feelings and the very marrow of its heart, and may have its beloved in its presence, not depicted but infused, not appearing but affecting," the Word "not striking the ears but seducing the feelings."[3] But even such absolute love of the absolute Being is transient. Half an hour, two hours — such are durations mentioned in mystical literature. The third degree is the eternal union of the soul and God in the beatific vision, described, again by Bernard, as "chaste and holy love, sweet and tender feeling, pure and flawless intention of the will, surely the purer and more flawless as there is now left no admixture of its own, the sweeter and more tender as all which is felt is the divine," and he adds, "to feel thus is to be deified.... The substance indeed will remain, but in another form, another glory, another power."[4] In these words the famous mystic emphasizes four aspects of the absolute experience: first, the sacrifice of freedom, when "there is now left no admixture" of the soul's own will; second, the eternal existence of the individual self, for "the substance indeed will remain"; third, the exclusive attention to God, when "all which is felt is the divine"; fourth, the perfection of the union, which can only be called deification.

Christian theology has a word for the union of God and man. The word is *Christ.* Christ is God and man, two natures in one person. Atheism is excluded, for Christ is God. Pantheism is excluded, for Christ is man. Sin is possible, for the natures are two. Sin is overcome, for the person is one. Christ is manifest in time, for he is not an abstraction. He is subject to the frailties of the flesh, being man, yet without sin, being God. The mystery of the incar-

3. Ibid., 31, 6.
4. Bernard of Clairvaux, *De Diligendo Deo,* 10, 28.

nation cuts across the rational system of nature. God, the Trinity, creation form a rational structure which philosophers may try to understand. But sin, the separation of man from God, and incarnation, the reunion of man with God, are non-rational facts. *Fact,* however, is not quite the word for these eternal mysteries. Existential and unintelligible, they are values rather than facts, situations rather than events, attitudes rather than descriptions. To the Christian Christ has a twofold practical meaning: Christ is his teacher, and Christ is his salvation.

To say that Christ is the Christian's teacher might be more significant in speaking to Hindus than in speaking to Americans. The Hindu's first loyalty is to his teacher or guru. The nearest thing to this in America is devotion to the Alma Mater, an incorporated guru, which is natural in a capitalist society, and an American seldom has any comparable emotional or financial tie to an individual teacher. But the Alma Mater is only a secular teacher, while the guru's teaching is also or primarily spiritual. India has an analogue of the Christian Bible in its Veda, of Christian theology in its Vedanta, of the clergy in its brahmins, of church buildings in its temples, but it has no analogue of the Church as an institution. The guru teaches on his own authority, not as part of an establishment. To a Hindu his guru, who by his own grace has taught him spiritual doctrines of supreme value, is entitled not merely to devotion and support but actually to worship, for his guru is the manifestation of God to him. Beyond the guru, however, as a still higher object of worship may be the guru's guru, called the *sat-guru* or true guru. For Christians Christ is the *sat-guru*. From him, through the apostolic succession, our immediate teachers have received their faith and their authority. Christ did not merely teach truths about God; the inspired prophets did that. He himself manifested God — "and we beheld his glory, the glory of the only begotten of the Father, full of grace and truth."

But Christ is also the Christian's salvation. I say salvation, not saviour. He is indeed the saviour, but he is this in his role as teacher. Any successful guru is the saviour of those whom he saves. But Christ is salvation itself. He is the union of God and man, which is salvation from sin, the separation of God and man. Christians are saved not only by Christ but in Christ. It is by becoming Christ, or, as they say, by becoming members of Christ, that they participate in the incarnation. They become members of Christ in baptism, and are nourished by the body and blood of Christ in communion. Whether the sacraments are interpreted as symbols or as effective miracles, they are already, symbolically or actually, the love of God. What remains is to perfect this love, to attain eternal and absolute Love of the absolute Being.

Such absolute Love is the highest good, justifying lesser goods as means to it, itself needing no justification. It cannot be reduced to hedonistic, cognitive, moral, or other values. Love is its own sanction, and seeks no good beyond itself. It cannot be justified, but it can be analysed. It can be defined in terms of ordinary experience. Analytical philosophers may be right in maintaining that significant ideas must be definable in terms of ordinary experience, but they are wrong in maintaining that metaphysical ideas cannot be so defined. Ordinary experience is always consciousness of a content. The consciousness and its content are experienced as distinct. Feeling is the uniting of the two, and absolute feeling or love is perfect union of consciousness and content with all separateness eliminated. As separateness is reduced, the subjective forms and categories which define finite phenomena are eliminated, so that love tends inevitably to become love of the infinite object, God. As the Renaissance neoplatonists put it, the lover is attracted first by the beauty of his lady's body, second by the beauty of her soul, third by Beauty as such, finally by God of whom Beauty is one aspect. But the object felt is never eliminated, so that the self is never freed from it, and the self which feels is never eliminated, so that the object is never freed from it. Absolute Love of absolute Being is the end toward which the process of purging the feeling faculty proceeds. It is the ideal of the Christian way, and Christians believe by faith that it is attainable. It is the Absolute beyond which there is nothing more. But it does not follow that absolute Love is the only Absolute. This brings us to a consideration of other religions.

# *Four*  Buddhism

WHEN I WAS A CHILD, A favourite toy was my roly-poly, a small Japanese doll rounded and weighted at the bottom so that, no matter how often knocked over, it automatically returned to its upright position. I did not know then that this doll represented Bodhidharma, the perfect type of imperturbability, who sat in meditation facing a blank wall for nine years and like the doll could be disturbed by nothing. Bodhidharma, the twenty-eighth patriarch of the Dhyana or Meditation School of Buddhism, brought the doctrine of this school from India to China in the year 520. His fourth successor Hung-jen, fifth patriarch of the school in China, as he drew near to the end of his life in 675, announced that *his* successor should be the one of his disciples who could prove that he best understood the doctrine. His scholarly disciple Shen-hsiu responded to this challenge by posting on the monastery bulletin board a stanza which can be translated as follows:

> The body is like the Bodhi-tree;
> The soul is like a shining mirror.
> Take care to keep the mirror clean
> And let no dust collect upon it.

The next morning a second stanza was found on the board:

> There really is no Bodhi-tree,
> Nor is the soul a shining mirror.
> As no such thing has ever been,
> How can the dust collect upon it?

This impertinent reply was the work of an uneducated woodcutter, Hui-neng, who had recently joined the monastery as a rice-pounder. The resultant scandal compelled him to leave, but later generations looked back to him as the author of the better stanza and so the real sixth patriarch and second founder of what we now call Zen. The issue between the man of learning and the man of insight was formulated in the stanzas. Is the soul like a mirror, or is it not a thing at all? The function of a mirror is to reflect, and of a clean mirror to reflect perfectly. If the soul is like a mirror, its function is to reflect reality, that is, know the truth. But if it is not a thing at all, it has no function, it cannot be soiled, and it cannot be cleaned. Which view represented the doctrine brought from the Holy Land of India by the imperturbable Bodhidharma? To answer this question we must first go back and consider Buddha himself.

India recently celebrated the 2500th anniversary of a man who, in view of the extent of his influence in space and time, might well be considered the most famous man in history. But what did Buddha do to be famous? He did not redeem mankind from original sin. He did not claim to be an incarnation of God, nor have his followers claimed it for him. He did not pretend to be a prophet inspired by God or an initiate transmitting esoteric science or a sage editing the wisdom of the ancients. His life, apart from legendary miracles, was that of a Hindu guru, and his doctrine was only to call attention to matters of common knowledge and ordinary experience. Tradition going back to his own time makes it possible to recover, under the mass of legend, a reasonably historical account of his life. Twice he scandalized his friends, in opposite ways. He was a royal prince, whose father, unsympathetic to the religious vocation evident from childhood, tried to keep him interested in secular life. The old raja was devoted and generous, but lacking in imagination. Whenever he noticed that his son was getting restless, the only thing he could think of was to get some more girls for the junior harem. The prince's decision to run away from home was confirmed as he made his way out, in the middle of the night, through the dormitory where the girls were sleeping—lying in inelegant postures, their night clothes in disarray, their cosmetics running, their hair in curlers, many snoring. This escape was the first scandal, scandalizing the court. Buddha joined a group of ascetics in the forest, where he devoted himself to their way of life, practising extreme asceticism in the old Hindu way. After six years of this he found he had made no spiritual progress, and furthermore he was hungry (as Christ was after only forty days), and he accepted some delicious rice pudding from the hand of a neighbouring farmer's pretty daughter. This was the second scandal, scandalizing the ascetics. Buddha then sat all one night under the Bodhi tree, and there he had the experience of enlightenment. Shortly thereafter he preached his first sermon, at Banaras, and here he stated those simple principles known to Buddhists as the Four Noble Truths: first, that life is suffering; second, that the cause of suffering is desire; third, that the elimination of suffering comes with the elimination of desire; fourth, that this is accomplished by following the path of right living and right thinking based on moderation and temperance. He devoted the rest of his long life to preaching, largely by parables. On one occasion, however, he sat in silence and held up a garland of flowers, to the perplexity of all the disciples except one, Mahakasyapa, who, it is said, suddenly smiled in perfect comprehension of this message.

The parables and other sayings of Buddha, as remembered by his disciples, formed a canon of Buddhist scripture handed down and eventually written in Pali. The history of Buddhism, like that of Christianity, is a history of many sects very different from one another. The type of Buddhism still dominant in Ceylon and Indo-China, called by its adherents the Way of the Elders and by its opponents the Lesser Vehicle, Hinyana, is a relatively simple application of the Four Noble Truths as interpreted in the Pali canon. The Greater Vehicle, Mahayana, which developed in northern India with a more scholastic literature in Sanskrit, has added an infinitely complex superstructure of mythology and philosophy, and the ideal of the compassionate bodhisattva who renounces his own nirvana to help others. The exotic and mystical Tantric Buddhism has flourished especially in Tibet. The coming of Mahayana Buddhism to China was a great crisis in the cultural history of the Far East, a greater crisis than that produced later by the coming of Western culture, which differed from Chinese culture much less than Indian culture did. Buddhist otherworldliness, celibacy, and meditation were radically incompatible with Chinese common sense, ancestor worship, and pragmatism. Partly through the influence of the native Chinese quasi-religious philosophy of Taoism, however, China adapted Buddhism to its own culture, and the various schools of Chinese Buddhism were further transformed when they were established in Japan.

In spite of the difference among the sects, it is possible to make some general statements about Buddhism, just as it is possible to do so about Christianity, with the understanding that the exceptions may be more widespread than the rules. Buddhism, like every religion, is a form of escapism. What we want to escape from is the suffering of this life. "Some have perverted notions, others have right notions, but all suffer the same pain," says the Lotus Sutra. Christians want to escape from sin, and it is only from heavenly messengers speaking through inspired scriptures that we can learn that we are in a state of sin, since the corrupt intellect cannot know its own corruption by itself. Vedantists want to escape from ignorance, and it is only from the Veda or the guru that we can learn that we are in a state of ignorance, since the blind cannot know they are blind unless told so. Hence the necessity of revelation in either case. But suffering is a fact of common experience, which we can ignore only by shutting our eyes to the obvious. Buddhism needs neither revelation nor esotericism. Its heavenly messengers are always with us. A Buddhist parable narrates that the King of Hell asked a newly arrived spirit whether during life he had met the Three Heavenly Messengers, and when he answered, "No, my Lord, I did not," he asked whether he had ever seen an old man bent with age or a poor and friendless sick man or a dead man.

The fact of universal suffering is the first of the four truths. The second truth, that desire is the cause of suffering, is true in the simple sense that frustration of desire is suffering in itself while fulfillment of desire produces further desire, but Buddhist philosophers have elaborated it in a subtle psychological study of causally related steps by which suffering and desire are connected. The third truth is that eliminating desire is the way to eliminate suffering, and the fourth summarizes the way of life by which our desires can be brought under control. This is simply the way of moderation and temperance. There are four ways of life: we can cause ourselves to suffer, cause others to suffer, do both, or do neither. Followers of the first way, it is said, are ascetics; of the second, the cruel and criminal; of the third, social reformers; of the fourth, those who, following Buddha's teaching, lead peaceful lives of kindness and wisdom. Disregard for social reform, an ideal so important for Christianity, is not peculiar to Buddhism but is characteristic of Indian thought in general, which considers social reform futile and meaningless. The Indian view of time, which is not a philosophical, religious, or scientific doctrine but a common sense way of thinking seldom questioned, contemplates time as infinite, the world as having no beginning, and society, although having cycles of development (which may be long by Western standards), remaining in the long run always the same. Humanity is not a species but a status. You can no more reform human society than you can educate the freshman class. Individuals, however, can be educated and reformed, and the goal of the discipline is release from the status. Buddhist ethics is personal, not social, although it is altruistic, directed toward other persons as individuals; even the ultimate ideal of saving all sentient beings from suffering does not envisage any reorganization of the social structure.

The Buddhist virtues are simply those of ordinary and universal morality, and these can usually be expressed in negative commandments, what "Thou shalt not" do. The first and greatest commandment is *ahimsa,* non-injury, not to kill or otherwise injure our fellows. Hence Asoka, the philosopher-king, who made Buddhism the state religion of his continent-wide empire, established renunciation of war as the basis of his foreign policy. But for Buddhists, who have not heard that man is made in the image of God, there is no sharp line between man and his fellow animals who are in a different status for the moment (or the aeon). *Ahimsa,* therefore, means non-injury and compassion toward all conscious beings, and Asoka also advocated vegetarianism, though he did not punish those who violated it. Unlike Western concern for the preservation of animals, which is aroused only when a species is threatened with destruction, Buddhist concern is compassion which recognizes the value of the individual — although in the long run the butcher (or meat eater), who cannot escape the consequences of his own acts, may be hurting himself more than he hurts the animal he kills. Other virtues are chastity, honesty, and temperance.

But in Buddhism, as in Christianity, those who take their religion seriously and are in a hurry to be saved become monks, that is, persons who follow not only the universal laws of morality but also the evangelical counsels of perfection. Buddhist monks, like Christian, take vows of celibacy and poverty. But there are two great differences. Buddhist monks do not have a vow of obedience, and the vows they do take are not irrevocable. Renunciation of personal freedom is the very heart of Christian monasticism, but a Buddhist monk never gives up his freedom.

This philosophy of life is an Epicurean-style philosophy of a highest good to be sought by any or all means, not a Stoic-style philosophy of a right way to behave regardless of consequences. There is no categorical imperative in Buddhist ethics. For Buddha the end justifies the means, even if the means involves telling lies — a point made in several of the parables (sometimes to the scandal, I find, of my more Kantian-minded students). One famous parable is that of the father who called his children out from a building on fire and, when they ignored him, called them to come get the toy carts he had bought for them, whereupon they came running. He did not have any toy carts, but he saved their lives. It is thus that the compassionate Buddha adopts whatever devices may be appropriate and teaches whatever doctrines may be effective, in accordnace with the various natures of the various persons he is concerned with saving, without regard to the intrinsic merit of the devices or the intrinsic truth of the doctrines.

Indifference to truth is still more apparent in Buddha's attitude toward speculative philosophy. There is no esoteric truth and no revealed dogma. Buddha stressed this in his last discourse, spoken when he was on the point of death. He exhorted the disciples to be "lamps to themselves," living by their own inner light, not relying on any external authority, even him. "Make of yourself a light; rely upon yourself; do not depend upon anyone else." From the Hindu point of view this means rejecting the authority of the Veda, and consequently Buddhists are not considered to be Hindus. But even the light of reason which we have within ourselves is not to be used for speculative philosophy. Buddhism is a practical way of life seeking freedom, not a theoretical system of knowledge seeking truth. Buddha repeatedly refused to get involved in metaphysical discussions, especially discussions of the four insoluble problems: Does the world have a beginning in time? Is it limited in space? Is the individual the self? Does the enlightened person still exist? To these questions one cannot truly answer either that it is so or that it is not so or that it is both so and not so or that it is neither so nor not so. None of the various answers recognized by Hindu four-valued logic is possible, because the questions themselves are illegitimate, being based on a false presupposition, the substantiality of the world or of the person. The analogy with Kant's antinomies is striking, and for Buddha, as for Kant, it is futile to argue about such pseudo-problems. But even if we could solve them theoretically, it would still be futile to do so practically. This point is made in the parable of the arrow. A soldier wounded by a poisoned arrow was taken to the Red Cross station, where a surgeon prepared to extract the arrow. But the wounded man stopped him. "Wait a minute, doctor. Before you begin, I want to know about this arrow. Is it made of rattan or reed, and from what kind of bird are the feathers? What kind of bow was it shot from, and was the bowstring of fiber or gut? Who shot the arrow, and what was his caste?" Before this information could be secured, the soldier would be dead. So shall we all be dead spiritually if we will not seek our salvation until we have learned all the relevant theological and metaphysical truths.

As might have been expected, it was futile to forbid the disciples to philosophize. Buddhism equals, if indeed it does not surpass, all other traditions in the extent and enthusiasm of its philosophical speculation and in the depth and subtlety of its philosophical theories. Still, the warning against metaphysics has been effective, and the Buddhist

philosophies have been analytical rather than metaphysical. Buddhism does not believe in God or the soul, those
two pillars of other religious philosophies. Experience reveals a world of infinite complexity, and scientific study
enables us to find some order and causal laws within this
world, but experience does not show us any eternal reality
underlying the phenomena. Neither experience nor
reason proves the existence of God, and we would never
even have thought of God except through the influence of
allegedly sacred or revealed scripture and teachers with a
vested interest in its transmission. The same applies to the
self or soul. Experience reveals a complicated variety of
conscious processes, and may suggest the occurrence of
unconscious ones also, but it does not show any self underlying this stream of consciousness. No experience either perceptual or introspective reveals any substance.
Substances, including God and self, are metaphysical fic-
tions not definable in terms of anything observed. Reality
is not substance but process, like a flame, which appears
to be a thing because it maintains a more or less constant
form, but really is nothing but a process, the stuff constantly changing, the form constantly renewed by causal
necessity. There is stuff, material of various kinds, and it is
constantly assuming new forms, but there is no enduring,
let alone eternal, substance.

For Buddhism as for all philosophy, "Know thyself" is
the first maxim, and the most important application of its
anti-metaphysical doctrine is in psychology. The Sanskrit
word for self is *atman*. The Buddhist view of self is expressed by the word *anatman*, "not self," which means
that there is no substantial self. The so-called self is merely
a process. It is a complicated process involving several
kinds of material stuff — physical matter, feelings (which
are a subtler form of matter), perceptions, volitions, and
underlying the others a still subtler kind of matter which
we can call consciousness. This is similar to, although
more complicated than, the Western psychological theory
which explains thinking as electricity, which is a very

subtle kind of matter but not immaterial or spiritual.

Like the matter in a flame, these five kinds of stuff are being constantly replaced as one process causes the next one. But there is nothing which endures except the sequence of events. Process is not substance. A substance can be contemplated, itself unchanged; it can be changed by acquiring new qualities, itself identical; it can be destroyed by a sufficiently powerful cause, ceasing to exist. But a process is always changing, is not identical with anything, and ceases of its own accord unless something keeps it going. The end of a process is not the destruction of anything. The classical Buddhist analogy for the *anatman* is a flame. The process continues so long as fuel is supplied and the temperature is maintained, and the flame itself produces the temperature needed to ignite the new fuel. If the fuel is exhausted or the temperature lowered, the process stops, and that is the end of the flame, but nothing is destroyed.

The waves of the sea provide an even more striking analogy. A wave may continue for a long time and may travel many miles, but the water does not travel. The whitecap on top of the wave is its most conspicuous part, but it is foam containing very little mass of water, and it is constantly ceasing and recurring, and in all these respects it is like the conscious mind. The body of the wave below the whitecap is less conspicuous but has more water and provides the matter for the foam — like the subconscious mind. The base of the wave is still more massive and it merges imperceptibly into the neighbouring waves and into the main body of the ocean, where, below the waves, most of the water exists — like the unconscious mind merging into the racial unconscious. Waves are pretty, but on the whole undesirable. The best thing to happen to waves is to have the wind stop blowing. The inertia of the water still maintains the waves for a while, but gradually they die down and the sea becomes smooth. The waves have been annihilated, but no water has been destroyed. The ocean has reverted to its natural state. In the case of those mental waves which we call individual selves, this natural state is nirvana. When the winds of desire which arouse the conscious processes by agitating the fivefold stuff cease to operate, the processes continue for a while through the inertia of karma, but gradually they die out.

The life process will never stop for lack of stuff. Like the fuel for a conflagration or the water for waves on the ocean, the psychic matter is inexhaustible. The conflagration will stop only if the temperature is lowered, the waves will stop only if the wind stops, and the mental process will stop only if desire stops. Normally the suffering produced by desire generates more desire, just as the flames produced by heat generate more heat. Positive virtue is not a solution: if bad acts have evil consequences, good acts have good consequences, and in either case life continues. Sensuous and ascetic desires are equally effective in maintaining the conscious process, and the follower of Buddha must imitate him in renouncing both. But the life of moderation, serenity, and compassion gradually permits our desires to lessen. Those who lead this life have a choice of three ways: the vehicle of disciples following the guidance of a teacher, the vehicle of hermits renouncing the world to live alone, the vehicle of bodhisattvas altruistically concerned with the salvation of others. According to the Lotus Sutra these three vehicles are the deer-carts, goat-carts, and bullock-carts by which the father lured his sons from the burning building, just tricks for turning men in the right direction. Really there is only one vehicle, the Buddha vehicle, enlightenment, which carries us across the stream of life to nirvana, the cessation of consciousness and suffering. Is nirvana annihilation or exaltation? This is one of the questions which Buddha refused to discuss. To ask what is the state of a soul after it attains nirvana is like asking what is the state of a fire after it goes out. If you ask, "Shall I cease to be if I attain nirvana?" the answer is *yes* if by *being* you mean to continue the suffering characteristic of this life, but the answer is *no* if by *being* you mean to be a substantial self, because you never were in this sense. The person who has attained nirvana, says the Buddhist patriarch Asvaghosha, simply "ceases to be disturbed."

Whatever nirvana is, non-being or super-being, it is at least clear what it is not. It is not continued existence as an individual. Whatever, if anything, is preserved in nirvana, individuality is lost. This fact presents a difficulty for persons brought up in the Western tradition, a difficulty which can be expressed by the question, "What's in it for me?" Setting aside all problems as to the truth or possibility of nirvana, why should anyone want nirvana? How can there be any value for me when I do not exist? Even in hell, with all its drawbacks, I shall at least continue to exist. Are we so attached to hedonistic values that we will give up being for fear of suffering? Is not nirvana, assuming it to be possible, simply an ultimate suicide? I believe that this question is a legitimate one. I do not think it can receive a straightforward answer, but an analysis of the question itself may help. There is a very real sense in which our basic concern is for ourself. As Rishi Yagnavalkya said in the Upanishad, "It is not for its own sake that anything is valued, but for the sake of the self."

The only thing which ultimately terrifies us is the threat of our own annihilation. Still, different people are terrified by different threats. To a small child there is nothing more terrifying than moving day, when the movers, big burly men, come right into his house, come right into his room, pick up his crib, his ultimate place of security, and carry it away. But to the adult this is not terrifying. He is probably moving to a better house, fulfilling a cherished desire. In any case he is moving to a different house. Whatever happens to the houses, it does not hurt him, because he does not, like the child, identify himself with house or furniture. So long as he lives, he exists. What terrifies the adult is death, and a criminal can force him to do anything by threatening to kill him, for he considers the destruction of the body the destruction of himself—that is, if he is a materialist. If he is a Christian, he does not fear

death; indeed he may even welcome it, because he iden-
tifies himself with the soul, not the body. He is willing to
leave his body as he is willing to leave his house, seeking
his true welfare in the experience of the soul. Only the
destruction of this could be ultimately terrifying, and that
is just why the notion of nirvana, when he hears of it, if
not frightening, since no one is forced to nirvana involun-
tarily, is at least dismaying. But the Buddhist does not
identify himself even with his soul, that is, his individual
mind, and so is not afraid to lose it, or may want to lose it.
To the question, "What's in it for me?" we can pose the
counter-question, "Just what do you refer to by the pronoun *me?*" The doctrine of *anatman*, not self, means that
the self is not the furniture or the body or the mind, is not
any of the five kinds of stuff into which Buddhist psychologists analyse the individual man. To lose these is to become free from them, not to be annihilated. The child, the
materialist, the Christian consider the loss of furniture,
body, mind to be annihilation. It all depends on what you
identify your self with. For the Buddhist, the true self,
whatever it is, transcends individuality.

This consideration of nirvana brings us back to Zen, and
to the poetry contest between Shen-hsiu and Hui-neng.
Zen has its own four principles: a special tradition outside
the scripture, no dependence upon books, direct pointing
to the self, enlightenment by intuition of one's own true
nature. According to Zen the scriptural canons of the various schools are only toy carts for motivating the completely unenlightened. The true teaching of Buddha was
not in writing or talking but in the silence which Saint
Mahakasyapa apprehended so well. While Hinyana and
Mahayana Buddhists studied their Pali and Sanskrit books,
he became the first patriarch of the Dhyana or Meditation
School, and handed down its traditions to his successors.
A thousand years later Bodhidharma, twenty-eighth in this
apostolic succession, perhaps foreseeing that Buddha was
destined to be disowned by his own people, brought the
tradition to China. Some Chinese philosophers were al-

ready enthusiastic Buddhists. The Chinese, great book lovers, were delighted by the Buddhist literature, and the pilgrims who went to the Holy Land did so chiefly to obtain manuscripts. But meditation was something different. Taoists, to be sure, liked to meditate, briefly, on landscapes. But Bodhidharma did his meditation facing a blank wall—standard practice in India but incomprehensible to the Chinese. The tension and conflict between the irresistible force of Bodhidharma's powerful personality and the immovable inertia of the practical Chinese temperament came to a climax a century and a half later when Hui-neng attacked Shen-hsiu's stanza. This stanza expressed the ideal of meditation. The mind must be kept pure like a spotless mirror, that is, perfectly passive and receptive, in order that the meditation may be undisturbed. Meditation is just what the practical woodcutter Hui-neng opposed. He substituted the ideal of sudden enlightenment for that of meditation, and this has remained the central principle of what we call Zen. He declared that "the truth of Zen opens by itself from within and has nothing to do with the practice of meditation." His successor condemned meditation as a hindrance to enlightenment. This is consistent with the ancient Buddhist view of the self as a process, like a flame, which goes out suddenly (though the simile seems inappropriate for enlightenment), but it is an historical paradox. The word Zen is simply the Japanese form of the Chinese Ch'an or Sanskrit Dhyana, meaning meditation. It is possible, therefore, to define Zen as "the rejection of Zen." The paradox is compounded by the fact that in Japanese practice the common method for attaining the sudden enlightenment opposed to meditation is prolonged meditation. But it is meditation with a difference. A standard technique in a Zen monastery is to meditate on some insoluble problem, not to sharpen the intellect but to discredit it. The meditation is terminated not when, as in Yoga or Christian mystical practice, it leads to union with its object but when it is rejected as absurd. Then the self is freed from thought.

The Zen master Hisamatsu Daisetzu, who was recently in America, expressed the central principle of Zen by a phrase which his translator rendered as "the Formless Self." This, I take it, is what is otherwise called nirvana. It is the self, but the self freed from all those forms which make it limited, definite, or individual. To realize the Formless Self is the purpose of the Zen discipline. To express the Formless Self is the purpose of the Zen arts. The realization is attained by enlightenment; rather, it is enlightenment. While other schools of Buddhism focus their attention on one or another of the vehicles, Zen aims directly at the one thing which brings about cessation of desire—enlightenment. We should not mistake the means for the end, but concentrate our attention on where we are going, not come to a halt revering the guide posts along the way. The intellect, which raises questions it cannot answer, is an impediment to enlightenment, the source of our dilemmas and existential crises. Life is suffering because of conflicting forces, and life is enigmatic because of conflicting concepts. Zen asks us to consider those simple experiences which cannot be expressed in words—the taste of a glass of wine, a moment of excitement at a sports event, the grass along the road where we are walking. "A primrose by the river's brim a yellow primrose was to him, and it was nothing more." It is the conceptualization of our experience which binds us, but we have grown so used to this that a great effort is required to recover the simplicity of the experience. A Zen writer, describing three trips along the same road, said: "The first time I just saw the grass and the trees; the second time I saw the glory of God shining through the grass and the trees; the third time I again just saw the grass and the trees." The more elaborate our philosophy or our religion, the more we are distracted from the Formless Self. When a Christian monk is peeling potatoes, he is doing it for the glory of God, but when a Zen monk is peeling potatoes, he is just peeling potatoes.

If the philosophy and discipline of Zen remain somewhat obscure to those of us brought up in other traditions, the expressions of Zen in art have a universal appeal. Whatever merits or demerits the Japanese may have in other fields, in aesthetics they are unsurpassed, and we turn to them for inspiration and instruction in the intuition and expression of beauty. For monks Zen means enlightenment, but for the world at large Zen means art. The Formless Self is expressed in the arts of poetry, calligraphy, painting, print-making, architecture, landscaping, interior decorating, flower arranging, dancing, wrestling, archery, and drinking tea. Knowledge of Zen philosophy may be necessary for understanding these expressions, but it is not necessary for appreciating them. We can admire a Japanese flower arrangement whether or not we have studied the theory involved. The theory, indeed, is difficult to formulate. Hisamatsu enumerates seven general characters of Zen art: asymmetry, simplicity, wizened severity, naturalness, dark subtlety, unattachedness, serenity. Japanese lyric poetry differs radically from the classical Chinese Taoist poetry to which historically it is related. A Chinese poem, by Li Po for example, compresses into a few words a tremendous amount of meaning, description, and emotion, so that the reader is strongly moved by the landscape described, the feelings, or the tragic situation. A seventeen-syllable Japanese poem does just the opposite. It expresses the least possible meaning, involves the least possible indication of the scene, and gives the least possible suggestion of emotion. It merely suggests or hints at a mood. It is up to the reader to elaborate the mood by his own associations, not those forced on him by the poet, so that not only the speaking but also the hearing is freely creative. For example, this poem by a Japanese emperor:

> When I went out in
> The Spring fields to pick
> The young greens for you,
> Snow fell on my sleeves.

Or this by a famous poet:

> *A strange old man*
> *Stops me,*
> *Looking out of my deep mirror.*

Or this:

> *No one spoke,*
> *The host, the guest,*
> *The white chrysanthemum.*[1]

Or this by a contemporary American Zen poetess:

> *Goldfish in the pond*
> *Lying quietly, sensing*
> *The rain's gentle splash.*

In each case the poet expresses his meaning not so much by what he says as by what he does not say. He is merely making a gesture, like Buddha lifting the garland of flowers. Likewise the Zen painter expresses his meaning not only by what he paints but also by what he does not paint. Zen art is just the opposite of the didactic Hindu art found in temples where every square inch of the building is covered by reliefs of mythological figures. Much of a Zen painting may be left blank, and the empty space may be the most important part of the painting, somewhat as the silence is the most important part of a Quaker meeting. The Quaker fills in the silence for himself, using the resources of his own Inner Light—filling it in not with words, however, but with silence. So the spectator must fill in the empty part of the painting not with forms but with the Formless Self. Zen disregard for books is illustrated by a popular picture of two legendary Taoist philosophers ridiculing the scripture. Most of the picture is blank, and this is the positive part. Ridiculing the scripture indi-

1. K. Rexroth, *One Hundred Poems from the Japanese* (New York: New Directions, 1955), 44, 24, 119.

cates only what you should not do, that is, depend on books. Screen paintings, the Japanese equivalent of Western murals, are especially well adapted for this, as a whole panel may be left blank, the formless panel expressing the Formless Self. Nevertheless, the figures which are painted, like the words of the poem or the flowers of the gesture, are indispensable. We are concerned here not with the ineffable and undepictable Formless Self in itself but with its expression in a formal medium. This is art. Meredith Blodgett, in a thesis on Zen written under my direction, includes a section on the expression of Zen in dancing based on her own experience. In this "formalisation of the Formless Self," she says, which because it needs no tools is perhaps the "fullest and most satisfactory expression," improvisation is to be rejected, as it "is likely to be ego-subjective and usually involves imagination and purposiveness." The dancer, like the painter, and for that matter like nature itself, must select a specific object through which his true Self can express itself. "The artist practices until he knows the dance perfectly. The pattern of movement becomes so natural to him that its performance no longer involves any thought whatsoever. . . . . The dancer now has an empty mind, and dances with a wealth of feeling which comes from beyond the ego."[2] In dancing, as in life, it is the conscious establishment of unconscious reflexes, habits, and disciplines which frees us from the tyranny of trivial decisions. But it is not necessary to be a professional or expert to be a Zen artist; drinking tea, the most common and ordinary act, if rightly performed, may express perfect enlightenment. Zen, perhaps more than any other Buddhist school, has upheld Buddha's principle that Buddhism is not a theory but a way of life.

Our concern in this book, however, is with the theory. Experience is a relation between consciousness and con-

2. M. Blodgett, "Zen Buddhism" (thesis, Tufts University, 1958), 74.

tent: in knowing, content determines consciousness; in willing, consciousness determines content; in feeling, each determines the other. Willing is the assertion of the subject. In knowing we submit to the object, and in feeling we unite with it, but in willing we determine what we want, and the objective world is changed accordingly, if the volition is successful. If what we know is truth and what we feel is love, what we will is freedom. In ordinary experience willing is imperfect and consequently freedom is limited. Insofar as we suffer, consciousness has failed to control even itself. Insofar as we desire certain objects real or imagined, will is dominated by those objects. Insofar as we know, will is adjusted to the knowledge. Insofar as we feel, will is directed by emotion. Suffering, desire, knowledge, and feeling accompany ordinary willing, but are incompatible with absolute willing. Willing is purged by the elimination of objectivity. Insofar as we will, we are indifferent to all claims of objects. Such freedom is the Buddhist ideal of serenity untroubled by objects, especially supposed substances, which demand either to be known or to be felt. When will rules desire instead of being ruled by it, there is no frustration and no suffering. Free of the objective world which he cares neither to know nor to feel, the Buddhist has an unassailable refuge in pure consciousness.

The ineffability of pure consciousness has its classical expression in Buddha's silence. It is also illustrated by the final examination and grades, so to speak, which Bodhidharma gave his disciples at the time of his own retirement: to one who said, "Truth is above affirmation and negation," he replied, "You have got my skin"; to the second, who said, "It is seen once and never again," he replied, "You have got my flesh"; to the third, who said, "There is nothing real," he replied, "You have got my bone"; to the fourth, who said nothing, he replied, "You have got my marrow." But its most impressive illustration, perhaps, is, paradoxically, a book, a book equally outstanding for profundity of meaning and elegance of style, a drama with

Buddha for its protagonist, eternity for its setting, the Absolute for its theme, the Lotus Sutra. The first part of this drama consists of praising the doctrine which is about to be declared. The last part consists of praising the doctrine which has just been declared. But the last part follows the first part without a break; there is nothing in between. The Absolute is always ineffable, but absolute Freedom is especially so. Truth is at least *known*, even if it cannot be formulated in words. Love is *felt*, which is something like being known. But Freedom is only *willed*. Absolute Freedom or nirvana, consciousness not determined by anything other than itself, the limit of the process in which willing is determined less and less by objects independent of it, cannot be made a content of consciousness, because that is just what it is not. In the first place, it means consciousness without content, subject without object, willing without willing anything, so that *will* becomes an intransitive verb. In relative willing we determine what we want, and object changes accordingly, but in absolute willing we want nothing, so there is no object. In the second place, it means self without individuality, either substance, which self never was, or process, which it ceases to be. We do not differ from each other by our consciousness; that is the fallacy of the substantial self. We differ from each other by the content of our consciousness, and where there is no content there is no difference and so no individuality. There is perhaps a more profound sense, at least so some Buddhist philosophers have taught, in which *samsara*, the phenomenal world of change and suffering, and *nirvana*, freedom from all change and suffering, are really identical, opposite sides of the same coin. So are the waves and the calm sea the same ocean. But for a person suffering from seasickness there is a practical difference. He does not need to be told that he is seasick, and he does not care to discuss its theory or have it explained that it is only mental, even if this be true; he wants the waves to stop. So all of us, in this life which is suffering, do not need a revelation to know we are suffering, and do not profit from metaphysical theories or from having it explained by the Vedantists that suffering is illusion, even if this be true, as some Buddhist philosophers have also taught. We want the waves of desire, which are the cause of suffering, to stop. This is accomplished not by knowing or feeling but by willing, and ultimately by absolute willing. Nirvana may be called annihilation or nothingness, since everything which can be conceived or pointed to is lacking. But that which cannot be conceived or pointed to, the will, still is, and because it is will it is active, acting on things in creative art and on men in compassionate charity, but not acted on. This is absolute Freedom, the state of Buddha and of every buddha, awakening without fixation. I spoke of Hui-neng, the woodcutter who wrote the second stanza, but I did not tell why he came to the Zen monastery. It was because he had become enlightened when he overheard a Buddhist priest reciting this verse from the Diamond Sutra: "Awaken the mind without fixing it anywhere."

# *Five*   Vedanta

HEN A SMALL NORTH Carolina college received a large endowment, the trustees set about making it into a great university, decided that its centre should be a great library, and resolved that over its door should be inscribed the motto *Truth Unfolds*, not in English or even Latin but in Sanskrit. They wrote a letter to Walter Clark, a scholar in that field, with the simple request that he translate *Truth Unfolds* into Sanskrit, adding in parentheses "like a flower." Professor Clark, however, refused to do so, replying that the notion of truth unfolding is so alien to the spirit of Indian thought that it could not be meaningfully rendered in Sanskrit. Truth is concealed and so must be unveiled, but it does not unfold like a flower. That Truth is unchanging and eternal is the first principle of Vedanta philosophy. To know absolute Truth is the final goal of Vedanta religion.

Vedanta, properly speaking, is the tradition based on the Upanishads, the philosophical portion of the Veda, and its central idea is that of absolute Being, called Brahman. It is not a religion or a theory but a group of philosophical schools, like Christian philosophy in the West, united by an historical tradition, respect for scripture, and certain categories of thought, but varied in content and capable of indefinite development. Its classical works are the ancient texts (Upanishads, Sutra, Gita) in which its basic ideas are set forth and the medieval commentaries in which its various philosophical theories are worked out, and it still flourishes today, with original works in English, the language of scholarship in modern India. The non-dualist (*advaita*) school of Vedanta teaches that Brahman is not merely the highest but actually the only reality. The so-called qualified non-dualist school is much like Christianity, teaching the goal of union with God in absolute Love (although its Indian way of thinking is exemplified by the detail that the perfect model of such love, analogous to the Christian Saint Francis, is said to be a monkey). And there are several other schools. In this book I use the word *Vedanta* as a convenient abbreviation for non-dualist Vedanta.

Vedanta, so understood, teaches that Brahman is the only reality and therefore the world, not being Brahman, is unreal and the self, being obviously real, is Brahman. The world, being not real but illusory, needs a psychological explanation for its appearance but no metaphysical explanation for its existence, because it does not exist in reality. Indian theologians say that God creates the world, and explain this as due to God's spontaneous and purposeless play, but this has only cosmological, not metaphysical, significance, for God also is part of the illusion. But even cosmologically, within the context of illusion, it is not correct to speak of the world as having a cause, because only events have causes, the so-called cause of a thing being the cause of its coming into being, while the world has existed forever and so never came into being and so has no cause. But, although the world has no beginning, it may have an end, indeed must have an end;

otherwise, like a dream from which one never woke up, it would not be illusion but reality. To escape from the world and its suffering, or more properly to bring the world to an end, is the practical, that is, religious, aspect of Vedanta. This does not require doing anything as in Buddhism or loving anyone as in Christianity but simply knowing the truth, for illusion is completely dispelled by knowledge. Vedanta is summarized in a simile attributed to Sri Ramakrishna:

> A little boy wearing the mask of the lion's head looks indeed very terrible. He goes where his little sister is at play and yells out hideously, which at once shocks and terrifies his sister, making her cry out in the highest pitch of her voice in the agony of despair to escape from the clutch of the terrible being. But when her little tormentor puts off the mask the frightened girl at once recognizes her loving brother and flies up to him, exclaiming, "Oh, it is my dear brother, after all!" Even such is the case of all the men of the world who are deluded and frightened and led to do all sorts of things by the nameless power of Maya, or Nescience, under the mask of which Brahman hides himself. But when the veil of Maya is taken from Brahman, the men do not then see in him a terrible and uncompromising Master, but their own beloved Other Self.[1]

The way to absolute Truth has five steps, which can be illustrated by the analogy of a boy seeking the truth about the first problem of cosmology, why does the sun rise. The first step is when the boy, observing this phenomenon every day, becomes curious and wonders why. His curiosity leads him to ask his father, who tells him that sunrise is an illusion due to the earth's rotation. He acknowledges his father's infallibility and consequently the truth of the answer, but he is perplexed by it, and this perplexity leads him to study astronomy in order to understand it. After he

1. R. H. Bucke, *Cosmic Consciousness* (New York: Dutton, 1923), 314.

has studied the proofs of the earth's rotation and the theory of diurnal motion, he understands the cause of the phenomenon himself, and is no longer dependent on his father's authority. The illusion continues, but as he concentrates on the scientific explanation, he gradually comes to see it in a new perspective. The observed phenomenon is the same, but he now sees the horizon going down instead of the sun coming up. When he grows up and becomes an astronaut, he goes off in a missile, from which, freed from his earthly point of observation, he sees objectively the earth rotating and the sun always shining. There is no longer any sunrise to explain. The illusion itself has ceased, not because anything objective has changed but because his way of seeing it has changed. The sun no longer rises, but only because it never did rise really. These same steps are to be followed in seeking the truth about the ultimate problem of metaphysics, what is real.

The first step toward absolute Truth is to *desire* it, or, to put it in the typically Hindu negative way, to desire to be released from illusion. Truth will not be forced on you against your will, indeed cannot possibly be attained without a strong desire. It might seem that truth is just what can be forced on you; you cannot be forced to will or to love, but you can be forced to perceive what is presented. Perception, however, is not truth but error. Nevertheless, perception provides the context in which truth is found. Vedanta is an empirical philosophy. It seeks truth not in logic or mathematics or an analysis of the concept of Being but in an analysis of experience. And by experience I mean ordinary experience; there is no mysticism in non-dualist Vedanta. This desire is not mere curiosity or wonder, because experience involves not only illusion but also suffering, and it is the suffering, which man naturally seeks to avoid, which provides the first motivation. There are, to be sure, other techniques for avoiding suffering, but according to Vedanta these are futile, because the suffering is also illusion, and illusion is overcome only by

knowledge. Desire for release from the illusion and suffering of ordinary experience is the most important of the
four antecedent conditions for philosophical study given
by the Vedanta philosopher Shankara, necessary qualifications for spiritual progress.

A second antecedent condition is self-control, understood in a comprehensive way as including control of
mind and body — self-restraint, patience in suffering,
contentment with little, serenity, attentiveness, faith,
mental concentration, discontinuance of superstitious
rituals, and the ordinary moral virtues. An immoral or
intemperate person cannot be expected to make even a
beginning in philosophy. For Vedanta moral behaviour is
not an application of theoretical knowledge but a prerequisite for it. Shankara's disciple Suresvara says: "Actions
cannot lead to freedom, which has to be accomplished by
knowledge alone. But . . . they are indirectly useful as a
means of preparing the ground for true knowledge. Thus
when a person, weary of the miseries of worldly life, has
his mind purified by the performance of obligatory duties,
the spirit of renunciation begins to operate in him."[2]

A third antecedent condition is renunciation of desire to
enjoy the fruit of one's action, either in this life or the
next — an ideal taught in the Bhagavad Gita, as also by the
Stoics and Kant, but the opposite of Buddha's Four Noble
Truths or Christ's Beatitudes. Duty, understood in the
Hindu way not as absolute but as relative to one's social
class and stage of life, is categorical, to be performed
purely as duty, not for some end. Desire for the fruit of our
action binds us to the world of illusion. Release is by
knowledge, not be deeds, even good deeds, which at best
have as their consequence pleasant illusions.

The fourth antecedent condition is ability to discriminate
between reality and appearance. The Chinese sage
Chuangtze once said, "Last night I dreamed I was a butter-

2. R. Das, *The Essentials of Advaitism* (Lahore: Banarasidas,
1933), 34.

fly; now I do not know whether I am Chuangtze who dreamed I was a butterfly or am a butterfly dreaming that I am Chuangtze." Shankara would never have accepted Chuangtze as a disciple. A man who cannot even tell whether he is awake or asleep can hardly be expected to make much progress in the search for absolute Truth. When we are dreaming, to be sure, we do not know we are dreaming, that is, not usually, just as in waking experience we do not know it is illusion, that is, unless we have studied philosophy. But in the experience of waking up we do know that the dream just ended was unreal, and that the waking experience is real relative to it, whether or not absolutely. It is the waking up from a dream, indeed, or the sublation of any other illusion, such as the snake seen to be a rope, which makes the notion of reality meaningful. If we never dreamed or had other illusions, it would be meaningless to call our waking experience real, and if we never woke up, it would be meaningless to call the dream unreal. The phenomenal world, likewise, can be called illusory only because, or if, it can be sublated in an experience analogous to waking up (and so Kant never called it illusory, as he recognized only the philosophical demonstration, not any intuition, of its unreality), and conversely the intuition of Brahman can be called Truth only because it is contrasted with an illusory experience, not hypothetical but actual, which has been sublated. And this is just why Vedanta must begin with perceptual experience. Truth is possible only by sublation of error. This quasi-supralapsarianism is inevitable in a religion of Truth. A person might always have been united with God in absolute Love or might always have enjoyed absolute Freedom (though both these statements can be challenged), but you cannot recognize Reality as real unless you have first experienced illusion.

The second step is to *know* the Truth. This is not difficult, as it is given in the revealed scripture, the Veda. At this stage, of course, it can only be believed by faith, which is a voluntary commitment, as it is not yet under-

stood by reason. The Vedanta notion of revelation is different from the Christian notion. The Bible is believed to
have been written at certain times by divinely inspired
prophets. The Veda is believed to be eternal and autono-
mous, a source of truth coordinate with experience and
reason, having no author human or divine, and for that
very reason infallible (as there is no author who might
have erred), just as infallible as experience, although like
it subject to fallible interpretations. But its function is the
same as that of the Bible in Christianity, to reveal truth
which unaided reason and experience cannot teach, although never to contradict what they do teach. Revelation
is the evidence for the existence of Brahman as the substantial Being underlying the world and Atman as the substantial Self underlying consciousness. To the Buddhist
who protests that experience discloses only processes and
that nobody would have even thought of Brahman or
Atman without revelation, the Vedantist can answer,
"Yes—but we do have revelation." As Suresvara said:
"Mere reasoning not only does not lead a man to his desired goal, but may also give rise to many undesirable
consequences. We have an example of its evil consequences in the case of the Buddhists who, disregarding
revelation, followed mere reasoning and came to the
theory that there is no self."[3] The Vedanta interpretation of
the Veda is summarized in three dogmas: beyond the
phenomena of perception is eternal Reality, Brahman;
beyond the stream of consciousness is eternal Self; Self
and Brahman are identical. This truth is expressed in the
mantra *Thou art That*, a formula which contains no nouns
or verbs or adjectives and therefore no concepts or conno-
tations, the personal pronoun *Thou* denoting the ineffable
Self, the demonstrative pronoun *That* denoting the ineffable Reality, and the copula *art* indicating their identity.
The revealed truths need not be learned directly by

3. Ibid., 97.

reading the Veda, but if they are learned from a teacher, he is revered as the immediate source of the individual's knowledge and instrument, by grace, of his spiritual welfare. A Vedantist who has a guru in the strict sense of acknowledged spiritual director and initiator (*gurudeva*, guru as God) both accepts the guru's teaching without question and depends on the guru's direction or at least permission for all that he does; that is, he renounces both intellectual and practical freedom.

The third step is to *understand* the Truth. Vedanta has the same problem of reason and revelation as Christianity, and Vedantists tend to adopt the Augustinian solution of faith seeking understanding. To know the Truth, faith is necessary psychologically but not logically. We cannot discover Truth without revelation, but having discovered it we can understand and demonstrate it rationally without any premise derived from revelation. Such understanding is Vedanta *philosophy*, based on pure reason apart from authority, but not abstract reason apart from experience. Philosophy is rational analysis, not of concepts, but of experience — not analysis of the content of experience, which is science, but analysis of the structure of experience. The first principle of such analysis is the distinction, given in experience itself, between consciousness and its content, subject and object, self and world, I and not-I. In practice we confound them, but in reflection we discriminate them. The object is known and contemplated. The subject is never an object, is not contemplated but enjoyed, and is not known except as knowing. Metaphysical arguments based on this distinction, epistemological arguments based on the conditions of perception, cosmological arguments based on the transiency of phenomena all lead to the conclusion that all objects are subjective and illusory and only the subject is objective and real. The self, not sublated in any possible experience, not eliminated in any possible analysis, not doubted in any possible scepticism, emerges as the reality beyond appearance, and recognizes itself as the real content of its own consciousness when all apparent content is analysed away. There are, to be sure, many controversial problems: Which comes first, ignorance or error? Does illusion exist because it is seen or is it seen because it exists? Is the person who has the illusion one or many? Is illusion itself real or illusory? Are there degrees of nonexistence? And in any case such analysis gives only speculative knowledge. It understands, but does not exorcise, the cosmic illusion. However, and here also Vedanta is Augustinian, just as believing the Truth is a prerequisite for understanding it, so understanding is a prerequisite for seeing it.

The fourth step is to *see* the Truth. We do not have to go to India to learn that the world of ordinary experience is not reality but appearance. This has been taught by Western philosophers from Plato on, most systematically by Kant. But we may have to go to India to find the theoretical and practical implications of this doctrine developed uncompromisingly and accepted seriously. Reality is not known in ordinary experience but, just because it is reality, it demands to be known, otherwise the knowing function of consciousness is frustrated. Kant rejected this demand, and maintained that reality cannot be known intuitively, but only speculatively or practically. Plato acknowledged the demand, but sought reality in abstract concepts, turning away from existential experience. The Vedanta sage, if this word can be used for one who goes beyond mere philosophy, makes a resolute effort to concentrate his attention on the reality in experience, to see Brahman in everything. This is meditation, but not like that of the yogi, who follows the way of willing with its physiological and psychological discipline, or that of the religious mystic, who follows the way of feeling with its ecstatic raptures. It is described by the Vedanta philosopher G. R. Malkani as follows:

Truth has not only to be found in experience, but it has also to be fully realized and lived. This is only possible by persistently checking the long-standing habits of wrong thinking, and keeping the mind fixed on the truth. It requires one-pointedness and devotion to a truth which we have begun to see intellectually. It removes the last impediment to a vision that will dispel ignorance for good. This is the only legitimate mysticism. Our rational faculties do not go to sleep. They are quite awake and alert. A mysticism based upon religious enthusiasm and the exercise of imagination or will is possible. But it has no theoretical value and is bound to be declaimed by reason.[4]

Such a person sees the same things as the rest of us, but evaluates them differently. He does the same things, but with a serenity which shows his freedom from illusion. He is free, but only in the sense that "the truth will make you free," that is, free from error. Neither saint nor Buddha, neither loving nor free, he lets his consciousness reflect its object as it is, and he sees that the object as it is is really the conscious Self.

The final step is to *realize* the Truth already desired, known, understood, and seen. The illusion vanishes, as a dream from which you awake. This consummation is not brought about by meditation but by a conversion of attention from the illusion which we already know to be unreal to the reality which we really know to be real. It does not involve any real change in the world, although it brings the world to an end, and it does not involve any real change in the Self, although it destroys the Self's individuality. The Self does not become Brahman. The Self always is Brahman, no less so if it does not know it, or rather if it does not attend to the Truth which it always does know. But from the point of view of the illusion, it is an event, and so must have a cause. We awake from a dream because of any of three causes: a violent stimulus, such as a loud noise, from the waking world intrudes into the dream and shatters it; or critical consideration of the dream expe-

4. G. R. Malkani, "Rational Intuition," *Philosophical Quarterly* (India), 28 (1955), 118.

rience from within shows that its fantastic content can be understood only as illusion, and this leads to awakening; or we wake up spontaneously after a short time, although it may be a long time as time is reckoned within the dream. It is the same with the cosmic illusion. We may be freed through an act of grace by God or an already released guru, a stimulus from the higher plane intruding into the lower one: this is the religious way. We may be freed as a consequence of understanding and seeing the world to be subjective and illusory: this is the philosophical way. We may be freed spontaneously, since illusion cannot last forever: this is the natural way. Suresvara, while recognizing the necessity of philosophical preparation, insists that the actual conversion of attention requires an external stimulus. He gives the analogy of ten woodcutters assembling to return home; one of them, wondering whether they are all there, counts and finds only nine, until someone reminds him of the fact, the obvious fact, that he is himself the tenth. "Just as the man, who looks for the tenth person beside the nine and feels distressed on not finding him there, comes to see the real state of things when he is told, 'Thou art the tenth' so does the enquirer after the Absolute arrive at a right knowledge of it when he is told by a proper person, 'Thou art That.' " [5] To know absolute Truth, all we need do is attend to the obvious, but psychologically this is difficult, because of the perverseness of the human mind characterized by original ignorance. While lying quietly in bed we attend to the fantastic images of our dreams, and when awake we attend to the equally unreal objects of perception, like Newton picking up pebbles on the beach, while the great ocean of Truth lies all undiscovered before us.

On the negative side, such realization is release from illusion (moksha). It eliminates all problems theoretical or practical. When you see a snake, you are perplexed and frightened. You have the theoretical problem of won-

5. R. Das, *The Essentials of Advaitism*, 110.

dering where the snake came from and the practical problem of avoiding being bitten. When you realize it is a rope, you do not *solve* either problem. You *eliminate* both problems: the snake did not come from anywhere, and cannot possibly bite you, because there is no snake, and never was. In the more common illusion of dreaming, if you are pursued by a bear, you may run—but he may run faster; you may climb a tree—but he may climb after you. The best thing to do is wake up, that is, stop being silly and attend to the obvious truth that you are lying safe in bed, and so realize not that the bear is gone but that there never was a bear. Even if you do not wake up, this is still true: you *are* safe in bed, whether you know it or not, and the bear cannot hurt you, no more can the snake even if you do not avoid the illusion. In the same way, since the objects of the world are only appearances, they and the terrors and pains associated with them can be escaped by realizing the truth, and even if you do not realize the truth it does not matter. There is no urgency about Vedanta. A Christian who does not love God risks eternal perdition, and a Buddhist who does not suppress desire risks unending rebirth, but a Vedantist who does not realize he is Brahman does not really risk anything. He is Brahman anyway.

On the positive side, realization of absolute Truth is enjoyment of bliss (mukti). Moksha and mukti are the same in denotation—to attain one is to attain the other—but different in connotation. To realize that you are really real is to realize that you are Brahman, absolute Reality. Unlike nirvana, which has no content, because it is consciousness without content, mukti has content, because it is content determining consciousness, even though the content turns out to be consciousness itself. In nirvana consciousness is undetermined; in mukti it determines itself. But how can ineffable Brahman be described? Vedanta philosophers agree that it has three attributes. First, Reality obviously is, and so has the attribute of *being*. As Parmenides pointed out in his true and profound, though perhaps inadequate, doctrine, Being is. Second, we know directly from experience that Reality is conscious, and so has the attribute of *consciousness*. As Descartes pointed out, I am obviously a thinking thing. Third, while we find life is suffering, as Buddha pointed out, as we advance in wisdom we find that our sufferings are associated with those aspects of life which critical analysis shows to be illusory, and we extrapolate to a reality free from illusion and therefore free from suffering, and say that Reality has the attribute of *bliss*. Being-consciousness-bliss is the description of Brahman insofar as it can be described philosophically. This is what the Self is, and what in mukti it realizes that it is. And it is one. The distinction of self and not-self must not be confused with the dualism of immaterial mind and material body in the Augustinian and Cartesian psychology of the West, with its perennial problem how they are related. Vedanta psychologists consider mind to be just as material as body, although made of a more subtle form of matter, like electricity in Western physiological psychology. They make a more elaborate analysis of the human person, however, as composed of matter in five states of increasing subtlety represented by solid body, vital breath, sensation, thought, and stream of consciousness. The Self or knowing consciousness is not to be confused with the mind or known content observed in introspection. Minds are just as diverse as bodies, and just as unreal. You and I differ from each other in our clothes, bodies, and minds, but these are what we have, not what we are. The Self which has them in your case and the Self which has them in my case are indistinguishable and therefore identical. Individuality is the primordial illusion underlying all other illusions. Nondualism is the absolute Truth conceptually described as being-consciousness-bliss. But this is only our human way of describing it. The literal, adequate, and accurate answer to the question, "What is Brahman?" is that *you* are.

In Vedanta as in other religions, the ethical problem of the obligation of the saved individual to help those not yet saved is controversial. In Christianity, Catholics expect the saints in heaven to intervene miraculously in the affairs of the living, indeed will not canonize them unless they do; Protestants do not. In Buddhism, Mahayana teaches if not the obligation at least the higher ethical opportunity of the enlightened individual to defer his own nirvana to help others attain theirs; Hinyana believes every man must work out his own salvation. In Vedanta four different views are found. (1) Some say that the individual freed from illusion (the *mukta*) gladly helps those still bound, presumably as a guru, like a Platonic philosopher going back down into the cave; "Having himself crossed the ocean of birth and death, he helps others to the shore of Immortality,"[6] says Swami Nikhilananda; some go so far as to say nobody should be a guru unless he is a *mukta*. (2) Others deny this; the *mukta*, like the wandering mendicant who abandons even wife and home for a life of perfect detachment, exists on a different level of being and need have no concern for those in the world to which he no longer belongs. (3) Others say that the very idea of such help is absurd: for the enlightened individual to want to help others, whose very existence he now sees to be illusory, would be like a man awakening from a dream wanting to go back to sleep again and recover the dream in order to help the persons he met there. (4) Others say that the problem never arises and so does not have to be solved; individuality is the very thing which we are saved from; therefore there is no saved individual and consequently no problem of a saved individual's duty.

Vedanta must not be confused with mysticism. That word is often used very loosely for any sort of abnormal experience, with a eulogistic or derogatory connotation depending on whether the writer likes or dislikes the unusual. Properly, mysticism means an ecstatic experience of loving God or any milder but similar feeling or any means

6. Swami Nikhilananda, *Self-Knowledge* (New York: Rama-krishna-Vivekananda Center, 1946), 110.

leading toward this end. It is characteristic of Christianity, Sufism, Vaishnavism, and Saivism. Yoga and Tantra have a pseudo-mysticism; their techniques are psychological rather than devotional, and their goal is freedom rather than love. Zen Buddhism and *non-dualist* Vedanta have no mysticism at all. Mystical ecstasy is transient, but Zen *satori* and Vedanta moksha are unique irrevocable changes of status. Mystical ecstasy is emotional, but Zen and Vedanta eschew sentiment and feeling. Mysticism has physiological symptoms; Zen and Vedanta, so far as I know, do not. Mysticism seeks sympathetic union of subject and object, to comprehend the object, and ultimately God the absolute Object, as united with the self. Zen and Vedanta seek on the contrary to comprehend the object as it is, but *as it is* has different meanings in the two cases. Zen just sees the grass and the trees, not the glory of God shining through them, that is, just sees them as phenomena produced by our forms of intuition and categories of understanding, with their primary and secondary qualities, determined by our human way of thinking, with consciousness determining content. It sees the object *as it is* but not *as it is in itself.* Vedanta seeks to comprehend the object more profoundly, that is, objectively, as thing in itself, with content itself determining consciousness. Christian art is devotional and sympathetic, Zen art is creative and imaginative, but non-dualist Vedanta as such is passive, expresses nothing, and has no art. Vedanta sees the world as a creature of God (as dualist Vedanta teaches), then as a manifestation of God (as qualified non-dualist Vedanta teaches), finally as illusion disappearing with the apprehension of Reality (as non-dualist Vedanta teaches). Truth does not unfold, but is unveiled, not gradually but all at once.

Hindus are more concerned with values than with facts. For Westerners the most fundamental category of thought is the distinction between fact and fiction, true story and fairy story, history and legend. We may consider whether Achilles should have dragged Hector around the walls of

Troy but we are more concerned with the question whether these persons existed actually or just in Homer's imagination. Hindus do not make, or at least do not emphasize, the distinction of fact and fiction. They are willing to argue the question whether Rama should have divorced Sita, but the question whether these personages existed historically does not arise. It is not that Indians are more superstitious or credulous; they do not think in these terms. They question Sita's divorce no more than they question Gandhi's assassination or Hanuman's leap to Ceylon or God's incarnating himself as a tortoise to serve as a pivot for churning the ocean. History, legend, myth, and absurdity merge into each other imperceptibly. In the West, the actual occurrence of a contemporary miracle must be conclusively proved before canonization, but the Devil's Advocate does not question its value, even if it seems trivial. Hindus discuss the value of alleged miracles, criticizing them as ostentatious or imprudent expenditures of spiritual energy, but do not question their actuality, even if the evidence is slight. This way of thinking may seem, but is not really, inconsistent with the description of Vedanta as search for Truth. It is tenable, indeed rationally inevitable, if life is illusion. When narrating a dream there is no point in distinguishing between what you truly did see and what you mistakenly thought you saw—though there is still a significant point in moral evaluation of what you did or aesthetic evaluation of what you saw. Actuality is not the same as reality. To ask whether Rama or the miracle actually existed is not a significant question. To ask whether they really existed is to change the subject to metaphysics. Of course they did not *really* exist; only Brahman is real.

Vedanta is the easiest religious way, because it requires doing nothing, yet the most difficult, for we have an instinctive urge to do something. Truth does not unfold; it is unveiled—but not really, for the veil also is illusory. As Gaudapada says, there is no suppression, no origination, no one in bondage, no one freed—this is the absolute

Truth.[7] We know when we accommodate our knowledge to that which is known — the opposite of willing. In ordinary experience our knowledge is perverted by wishful prejudices arising from will and emotional biases arising from feeling. The seeker of Truth must purge his knowing of all will and all feeling, of all subjective influences, so that only that which is objective, that is, real, remains. This is just what the scientist does in his unprejudiced and dispassionate exploration of reality. But the scientist does not carry out the project thoroughly. Science is controlled by a priori subjective forms of intuition and categories of understanding, as Kant pointed out, and insofar as the scientist is satisfied with these, satisfied to apprehend the world in time and space and understand it in terms of causality, he stops short of the search for pure knowledge of objective reality. The mystic goes further, finding the world eternal and immaterial because he has freed his intuition from the subjective forms of time and space, and ineffable because he has freed it from the categories of understanding. But the mystic turns aside from the search for truth in his zeal for love, seeking not to be like a mirror reflecting God as the Absolute but like a bride united with God in love. The Vedantist refuses either to abandon the ideal of absolute Truth with the scientist or to turn aside from it with the mystic. Absolute Truth is attained when and if experience is purged of all subjectivity. The subjective is false, and all objects are subjective. The only thing which is not subjective is the subject itself. Professor Malkani says: "Ultimate reality in itself has no character whatsoever. A character implies objectivity, and ultimate reality is no kind of object. We may therefore enumerate all its so-called characters, but that cannot enable us to know it as it is. The only thing that can so enable us is its character or want of character that is implied in the assertion of its identity with the Self. Ultimate reality is ulti-

7. Gaudapada, *Agamasastra* II, 32 (University of Calcutta, 1943),39.

mately nothing but the Self.''[8] The Self is not something beyond experience. It is given in all experience, and is always known — not known, like an object, by perception, introspection, understanding, or any sort of contemplation, but known as knowing. ''The self is nothing but experience itself,''[9] says Suresvara. Absolute Truth, which is absolute being, consciousness, and bliss, is experience purged of all subjectivity in pure knowing. It is not realized by any individual, for illusory individuality is destroyed, along with the phenomenal world depending on it, though destroyed only in the sense that it never really was. Desired by the disciple, known by the believer, understood by the philosopher, and seen by the sage, absolute Truth is realized as Self knowing Self by being Self.

8. G. R. Malkani, *Philosophy of the Self* (Amalner: Indian Institute of Philosophy, 1939), 2.
9. R. Das, *The Essentials of Advaitism,* 65.

# *Six*  Commitment and Coexistence

HE WORLD IS ONE, BUT there are many paths leading from it. There are, to be precise, three paths. A religion is a way of escape from the world, and consequently there are three types of religion. This conclusion is not derived inductively from a consideration of the various religions but deductively from a consideration of the world. The world is what is known in ordinary experience, which involves consciousness and its content. There are three ways in which they can be related — content determining consciousness, consciousness determining content, both determining each other; and these are the conscious functions knowing, willing, and feeling. Ordinary experience, that is, the world, is a mixture of them — a mixture, not a synthesis, because as mutually contradictory and incompatible they cannot be synthesized. It is characterized by ignorance because knowing is not pure, suffering because willing is not pure, and sin because feeling is not pure, each being modified by the others. Escape from the world, that is, from this mixture, is accomplished by a psychological abstraction which abstracts one function from the others, taking the one and leaving, that is, giving up or sacrificing, the others. There is no necessity to do this. Instead of ordering either steak or chicken or lobster you can have steak-chicken-and-lobster hash made from the leftovers. You can keep all three functions, remaining in the world and renouncing religion. But if any one function is partially purified, you are leaving the world, and if it is perfectly purified, it is completely freed from the others, and these three perfections are the alternative forms of the Absolute, which are the alternative goals of religion. There are four possibilities, to stay in the world or follow any of the three paths. To stay requires doing nothing, as we are already there. To follow any way requires commitment to it. To follow more than one and so seek incompatible goals leads to religious frustration.

Christianity, Buddhism, and non-dualist Vedanta are examples of the three types. Other religions, whether in the same cultural traditions or not, offer other examples. Vaishnavism, in the same cultural tradition as Buddhism and Vedanta, is a religion like Christianity, with its goal union by love with the personal God. Islam, in the same cultural tradition as Christianity, is a sort of Hinyana Christianity, with relatively simple theology, ritual, and organization, but the same goal of loving God. Christian Science and Vignanavada Buddhism are like Vedanta, seeking truth by rejecting illusion, but not going so far; they teach that matter is illusory but not that mind is also illusory. Jainism, with its impressive ethical and logical teaching, is nevertheless imperfect as religion, refusing to sacrifice any of the three values and consequently failing to attain any of them absolutely, and indeed the Jains call their philosophy "non-absolutism." For Jains the ideal of knowledge is mere omniscience, detailed knowledge of the phenomenal world, not metaphysical Truth; the ideal of freedom is mere bliss, freedom from suffering and rebirth, but not from individuality; the ideal of love is mere charity, not union with the loved object, although in extending charity to all living beings Jainism does offer a norm of perfect morality. Taoism, with its anti-scholastic indifference to truth and unsentimental disregard for love, seeks freedom like Buddhism, in a different cultural tradition, but not absolutely, seeking freedom from the cares of the world but not from the world itself, freedom from death but not from life. Confucianism is not religion at all.

Religion must not be confused with morality or altruism. They are of course closely related. By good works "a lively faith may be as evidently known as a tree discerned by the fruit," it says in the Thirty-nine Articles. A saint, arhat, or *mukta* is not apt to behave immorally (though Hindu legend knows of irascible hermits spiritually advanced but socially unpleasant). Still, morality is neither a necessary nor a sufficient condition of religion. Confucius is the type of moral but irreligious man, David the type of religious but immoral man. Christianity teaches that moral sins are forgiven by religious techniques; only the sin against the Holy Ghost is unforgivable, not any sin against man, no matter how serious; moral delinquencies do not condemn you to hell, only the religious delinquency of separation from God. Buddhism teaches that good desires are no more effective than evil desires for spiritual progress, which requires cessation of all desires. Vedanta teaches that the enlightened man transcends the distinction of good and evil which is valid only in the context of illusion. Altruism is optional in religion: Franciscans are devoted to serving others; Carmelites concentrate on their own spiritual perfection; Benedictines seek to balance the two by combining the active and contemplative lives (Martha and Mary, Leah and Rachel). Morality is not an end in itself for religion. The Christian saint performs works, or even miracles, of mercy for the glory of God. The Buddhist bodhisattva may help others to enjoy life (letting a hungry tiger eat him, for example), but his purpose and vow are to help others escape from life. The Vedanta philosopher performs good deeds, if at all, as a prerequisite for knowledge. War is advocated by Vedanta in theory, by Christianity in practice, and by Islam in both. The act of the liberal Emperor Frederick II, who fulfilled his crusader's vow by diplomacy which gave him Jerusalem without bloodshed, can only be applauded on moral grounds, but of course it did not get him canonized; Dante met him in hell but found Godfrey, leader of the earlier bloody capture of that city, in heaven. A belief that religion and morality are equivalent results from the fallacious argument that, since both are good, a man who has one is a good man and so must have the other.

It does not follow, however, that religion should be rejected on moral grounds, as the Communists would have us do. Religion is not the opiate of the masses; "They chose atheism as an opiate," is Webster's example in defining that word. Religion is the great stimulant. Even if we accept the dubious premise that love for our fellow men is the most important thing, a premise which inverts the order of the two great commandments, it does not follow that religion should be rejected or ignored. If religion and morality are not equivalent, they are positively correlated statistically. It is a paradox that the materialists who believe that this short life is all we have, and might logically be expected to do everything possible to make it dignified and beautiful, in practice often make it cheap and sordid, while those who believe this life to be a pilgrimage, and might logically be expected to ignore its transient goods, in practice have been most active in works of charity, social reform, scholarly research, and creative art. The influence of Christianity mitigated the horrors, especially slavery, of ancient Rome, and religiously motivated persons led the attack on slavery when revived in modern times. Buddhism brought a softening humanitarian and compassionate influence to overcome the cruel and heartless customs of pre-Buddhist China. Religious emphasis made later Indian society very different from the secular totalitarianism described in the ancient Classic of Politics. Nevertheless, the exceptions to this rule are so overwhelming as to jeopardize the claim of religion to any moral value at all. Religious wars, persecutions, and inquisitions are one of the darkest blots on the history of civilization, and at times have been a dominant characteristic of society, notably in India during the last millennium. They are the scandal of religion, a scandal so great as to make it seem the world might be better without religion. But these atrocities are caused, not by religions themselves, with their invariably humanitarian teachings, but by the fanatic dogmatism of alleged orthodoxy insisting that its way is the only way, and its goal the only goal, which must be accepted by all. Religious wars and persecutions are due to the clash of opposing religions. Persecutions are not against the irreligious but against heretics or infidels, that is, adherents of other religions, whether individuals, groups, or nations. The torment of India has been caused by a dogmatism which has made religious coexistence impossible. The solution is not liberalism. The liberal emperor Akbar undertook to heal the division among his subjects by playing down both Islam and Hinduism in favor of a new innocuous religion based on the simple principles of liberality, beneficence, and unitarianism, with himself as its head. Its spirit is expressed in a temple inscription:

> O God, in every temple I see people that worship thee,
> and in every language I hear spoken people praise thee.
> Polytheism and Islam feel after thee. Each religion says,
> "Thou art one, without equal." If it be a mosque,
> people murmur thy holy prayer, and if it be a Christian
> church, people ring thy bell from love of thee.
> Sometimes I frequent the Christian cloister and
> sometimes the mosque. But it is thou whom I search
> from temple to temple. Thy elect have no dealings with
> either heresy or orthodoxy, for neither of them stands
> behind the screen of thy Truth.[1]

1. M. L. R. Choudhury, *Din-i-Ilahi* (Calcutta: Dasgupta, 1952), 197.

Nothing came from this well-intentioned project of the great and good emperor either religiously, for this is not how religions are founded, or morally, for it lacked the enthusiasm of commitment. Very different was the reform accomplished two thousand years earlier by his great predecessor Asoka, who definitely committed himself personally to Buddhism in its fulness and made it the state religion, at the same time encouraging and supporting all other religions in a spirit not of liberalism or tolerance but of coexistence as alternative faiths. At Akbar's death his empire continued but his reform perished; at Asoka's death his empire collapsed but his reform had a profound and lasting influence on India and the world. The emperors Asoka, Akbar, and Aurangzeb ruled India with religious coexistence, liberalism, and dogmatism respectively; all were great emperors and religious men, but Asoka was also wise. At Akbar's tomb, however, the spirit of alternation and commitment speaks today in the sign at the door, "Visitors are requested to remove either their hats or their shoes"; a dogmatic sign would say, "Shoes off"; a liberal one, "No special gesture required."

The various religious ways are alike in awakening the mind but different in where they fix it. The way of Christianity is to awaken the mind and fix it on God; that of Vedanta, to awaken the mind and fix it on the Self; that of Buddhism, to awaken the mind and fix it nowhere. They cannot be integrated, because they fix the mind at different places. They cannot judge one another, because they have no positive ideal in common. But they are alike in aspiration, although not in the object of aspiration, and they can agree in opposing irreligion. Their attitude toward each other should be neither dogmatism nor tolerance nor liberalism but coexistence.

Religious life is languishing in the world today. Intellectual life, on the contrary, is flourishing as never before. That is because our intellectual life is based on coexistence. In a university, the professor of chemistry, who may know and care little or nothing about history, does not dogmatically attack and try to expel the professor of history on the ground that chemistry is the only subject worth studying. He does not tolerantly accept him as someone whose activity he must allow but need not approve. He does not liberally pretend that they are both doing the same thing in different ways, and so propose a curriculum based on the history of chemistry. He respects his colleague as someone who is doing something quite different, something which he personally does not care to do, something which can neither be evaluated in terms of chemistry nor joined with it in any comprehensive summary, but something of alternative value. The student is not dogmatically obliged to follow a fixed curriculum as he was a century ago, or liberally permitted to enjoy a free elective system as he was somewhat later, but is required to choose a major, to choose it freely, and having chosen it to pursue it in depth, at the same time learning to respect other subjects without attempting to master them. A technical institution may teach one thing well, but does not give an education. On the other hand, it is possible to give a course on things in general (I once did myself, and it was pretty thin) or a four-year liberal curriculum based on the Hundred Great Books, but this is not what has made our country intellectually great. Academic coexistence means on the one hand that the chemist follows his own commitment singlemindedly, and on the other hand that he cooperates with his colleague the historian in the administrative affairs of the university and in fighting their common enemy, which is the ignorance and apathy opposed to all education. A university is not bound together merely by a central heating system, but by coexistence of disciplines. This is the bond of the university and the strength of the intellectual life of our society.

Coexistence, which avoids both the destructiveness of dogmatism and the poverty of liberalism, is important in many fields of life. In international politics disaster is imminent, with a threat of unprecedented devastation, as the nations strive dogmatically to impose their own political systems on each other, instead of coexisting in mutual respect on a planet big enough for alternative ways of life. It would be also unfortunate, though less violent, and certainly very unlikely, if the progress in social welfare made possible by strong government should be undone by the various governments' liberally becoming alike through reducing their activities to the bare essentials of a *laissez-faire* system. Our concern in this book, however, is with coexistence in religion. There may have been times and places where isolation made this less important, although even in a relatively isolated and religiously homogeneous society like medieval Christendom the dogmatic urge to persecute the heretic within and crusade against the infidel without was irresistible. But today there is no isolation. The modern acceleration of transportation and communication has not made the world one. It has emphasized how manifold the world is. Religions can no longer ignore each other. But they do not have to fight each other because of their differences or abolish their differences to avoid fighting. Religion is concerned with man's ultimate goals in this life and beyond. It would be a catastrophic disaster to civilization at this time of worldwide communication and intercourse for the great religions to destroy each other either by dogmatically attacking each other or by liberally merging into some watered down world religion. Christianity must distinguish between its friends and its enemies. Its enemies are secularism and humanism. But its friends are Buddhism and Vedanta and Islam. In the world today they must live together as alternative religions or else they will perish together, because there are powerful forces opposing religion as such.

Religion is otherworldliness. Its opponent is thisworldliness. The greatest enemy of any and all religion is secularism. Communism is the extreme form of this, but ordinary American secularism is almost as dangerous. The competitive lure of secular activities—which may, to be sure, provide for the welfare of the body and the impressive paraphernalia of an affluent society—can destroy the Church no less surely than violent persecution. A second enemy of religion is humanism, the principle that man is good by himself without any supernatural aspiration. Humanism attracts the broad but shallowminded man, appealing at once to his pride, his altruism, and his freedom from superstition. Historically the most elaborate manifestation of humanism has been Confucianism, with its basic principle that man is by nature good, and it is in accordance with this principle that Confucian scholasticism has never felt any need for religion but only for a systematic formulation and application of innate goodness. Confucianism has not sought love of God— rapport with Deity is the concern of the Emperor alone; or freedom—to fit into the social structure is the ideal; or otherworldly truth—"not knowing life, how can I know death?" asked Confucius. As humanism, to be sure, it is superb, and we may well agree with Giles that "never, perhaps, in the history of the human race has one man exerted such an enormous influence for good on after generations."[2] A third enemy of religion is pseudo-religion organized as a Church and preaching the social gospel. The social gospel is of course essential to Christianity, but the priorities were explicitly declared by Christ when, in a formal answer to the question, which is the first commandment of all, he stated that to love God is the first and to love your neighbour the second. Secularism, communism, humanism, and the social gospel have all contributed to make this world a better world. But insofar as they lay claim to our highest loyalty they are implacable enemies of Christianity or any other religion.

Any religion, with its commitment to the Absolute, should be strong enough to stand against the outer forces of secularism. It can hardly expect to convert all men, but it can maintain its otherworldliness in a thisworldly envi-

2. L. Giles, *The Sayings of Confucius* (London: Murray, 1907), 118.

ronment, like a monadnock of granite rising from a plain. The greater dangers are the inner forces of the logic of *not* and the logic of *and*, dogmatic orthodoxy and shallow liberalism. The attitude of the different religions toward each other, when they do not ignore each other, an evasion becoming more and more difficult, has been either dogmatic, attacking each other ideologically and even physically, or liberal, accepting each other as somehow equivalent. Both attitudes are fraught with disaster, the former threatening mutual destruction like the annihilation of both armies in the Kurukshetra War (an annihilation accompanied by loss of moral integrity), the latter leading to the withering away of religions as everything incompatible with the others is eliminated, either attitude leaving secularism triumphant.

The present situation, however, is the opposite of that in politics. In the world today, and the foreseeable future, there is little danger that governments will wither away, but great danger that they may violently destroy each other. In religion, on the contrary, there seems little immediate danger of serious religious war, either a war of bombs (though religion might be used to rationalize a war motivated politically) or a war of words. People do not take religion that seriously. Missionaries are mostly medical or teaching missionaries. Even the most elementary aspect of religion, concern with and preparation for death, is unfashionable. The former Victorian taboo on sex has been succeeded by an equally unhealthful taboo on death, which is just as natural and even more inevitable. We do not talk about it, perhaps because, as the existentialist philosophers point out, it is the fact which makes our secular ideology absurd, and even those who wish to talk about it are inhibited by its being bad etiquette to do so. The danger today is fashionable liberalism, to oppose which is almost a breach of etiquette. Ecumenicity, either within one religion or among all religions, is good insofar as it means, on the one hand, cooperation with other faiths in their common concerns of social activities and resistance to irreligion, and on the other hand, mutual respect for the other faiths themselves. But it is bad when it degenerates into liberalism, which pretends to embrace various religions in their religious aspects. The great spiritual teacher Sri Ramakrishna did practise different religions, but only one at a time. Conversion within a religion may be progressive, as a Hinyanist might become a Mahayanist or a Protestant a Catholic by adding something, but conversion to religion of another type is possible only by starting over, as you can go from one mountain to another only by way of the valley. A religious person can appreciate another religion better than an irreligious person, as a man on a mountain can see another mountain better than a man in the valley, but a person can embrace two religions only at their lowest levels, as a person can plant his two feet on two mountains only at the lowest point of the valley. A person following one type of religion cannot also follow another type. This is not because one requires all his energy, like vocations, which are incompatible only in practice, not in theory, so that an individual who is a genius may have two, like Schweitzer both musician and doctor. Religions are incompatible in principle. Liberalism, which denies their incompatability, is possible only by reducing the religions to a bare minimum in which the essence of each is rejected and so essentially they cease to exist. But religions which do not exist cannot coexist, either in the individual or in society. Gandhi, a great liberal, said, "Religions are different roads converging to the same point," and asked, "What does it matter that we take different roads so long as we reach the same goal? Wherein is the cause for quarreling?"[3] I ask: What does it matter that we reach different goals? Wherein is the cause for quarreling?

The psychological causes of the dogmatic and liberal attitudes are doubtless complex, but their philosophical rationalization is the same in both cases, namely, the pre-

3. M. K. Gandhi, *Hind Swaraj* (Ahmedabad: Navajivan Publishing House, 1938), 36.

supposition of monism. The problem raised in introductory philosophy courses, "What is the summum bonum?" is a remarkable example, though seldom remarked, of the "fallacy of many questions," presupposing in a question asked the answer to a question not asked. In speculative philosophy there is an established tradition, at least as old as Parmenides, that the Absolute must be one. Pluralists who reject the theory of one Absolute express their doctrine by denying any absolute rather than by asserting a plurality of absolutes. That "there is at most one God" (Whitehead's definition of Unitarianism) is accepted by both monists and pluralists. In religion, which is concerned with values, monism means that there is only one absolute value, a thesis generally accepted although demonstrably false. Hence the person seeking the Absolute in a way different from your way is either wrong or else not really different. The most common argument for the oneness of the Absolute, if it is questioned, is that to be one is part of what we *mean* by the Absolute—which is no argument at all. Like the ontological proof, which demonstrates the existence of God by defining the concept of God to include existence, this anontological proof demonstrates the nonexistence of alternative absolutes by defining the concept of plural absolutes as including nonexistence. It is often put, not that the Absolute *is* one but that the Absolute *must* be one; it is a common English idiom to use this modal form to express a conclusion emotionally stressed because rationally indemonstrable. (Life *must* have had a beginning, but nobody says that two and two *must* be four.) It may be that God is one, that absolute Freedom is one, that absolute Truth is one—at least the present argument does not question these assertions. But the Absolute is many. This cannot be refuted by arguing that plural absolutes would limit each other and so not be absolute. Logically, this is indeed the point. *Absolute* Love, Freedom, and Truth, being radically different and incommensurable, with nothing positive in common, do not impinge or encroach on or in any way limit each other. Only *relative* love, freedom, and truth — relative, partial, or imperfect just because mixed with each other — can be associated with and therefore limit each other.

Being is a metaconcept comprehensive enough to include all concepts, and we can say that Absolute Being is the one Absolute which comprehends all absolutes, but it does not follow that this saying has any significance either theoretical or practical. It could be given significance only by a transcendental criticism of all philosophies and religions. An elaborate attempt to accomplish this was made by that greatest of dialectitians the second century Buddhist philosopher Nagarjuna. His "transcendental wisdom" is based on a critical examination of philosophical systems. Reflection on the opposition and alternation between the various systems proceeds dialectically to realization of the inconsistencies intrinsic to all and awareness of the indefinite reality which underlies all, ultimately to the absolute Indefinite free from both being and nonbeing, the last word of philosophy, the negation of all views, and the beginning of a higher wisdom best expressed by silence. This absolute Indefinite is just the opposite of Plato's absolute Good, apparently unintelligible because its excessive intelligibility dazzles the intellect, or Hegel's absolute Idea, further indefinable because including all definitions. Here we have a fourth logic besides the logic of this *not* that, this *and* that, and this *or* that, a logic of *neither* this *nor* that, road closed both ways, co-nonexistence. Even if this subtle and profound philosophy, alleged to be the esoteric teaching of Buddha entrusted to the Nagas and hidden for eight centuries, be accepted as somehow ultimately right, it is beyond either a theoretical philosophy or religion which can be believed or a practical philosophy or religion which can be lived. But is it ultimately right? The absolute Indefinite seems rather to be the ultimate consequence following by uncompromising dialectic from the false axiom that the Absolute is one. At best it is justified by reason. But the exis-

tentially oriented and phenomenologically grounded
doctrine of alternative goals is based on experience.

Coexistence, that is, the recognition of alternatives, is
what makes commitment possible, in religion or in anything. Liberalism, the denial of differences, makes commitment impossible, because the vestigial religion left
after rejecting the differences has no significant essence.
Liberal Christianity may teach the fatherhood of God and
brotherhood of man (hardly religion, let alone Christianity), but a generalized liberalism must reject even the
former through deference to Buddhism, which denies
God, and the latter through deference to Vedanta, which
denies human individuality. But dogmatism also makes
significant commitment impossible. If it is based on ignorance of alternatives, there is no choice and therefore no
commitment. If it is based on contempt of alternatives, it
denies others the right to commit themselves. It is only in
the context of coexistence that authentic commitment is
possible, commitment to something significant (as against
liberalism) and made freely (as against dogmatism), commitment in depth, which determines what we ourselves
become. It is not the unexamined life which, as Socrates
said, is not worth living, but the life without commitment.
How far religious commitment proceeds depends on the
person's capacity. In principle it may proceed all the way
to the Absolute.

Capacity, however, means religious, not intellectual,
capacity. Fra Angelico's painting of heaven shows serious
looking saints mounting upward and passing on the way
lesser saints who are frolicking with angels (presumably
lesser angels) in flowery fields. The suggestion is that some
saints have the capacity to proceed to the Absolute while
others go only part way. This may be so, but we should be
cautious how we interpret the concept of capacity, re-
membering the theological cliché that a small cup filled
with wine, although holding less wine than a large cup, is
still just as full. In any case, we should be careful what we
identify capacity with. Intellect is no more necessary than

money, useful as these are for other purposes. Jesus said you can enter the kingdom of God only as a little child. The French mini-saint Teresa of Lisieux cannot compare with her great Spanish namesake in intellectual ability or mystical insight but somehow seems no inferior in sanctity, that is, in the purity of her love of God. The naive Vaishnava saints Chaitanya and Mirabai do not have the literary genius of Tulasidasa but seem equal to him, so to speak, religiously. The woodcutter Hui-neng grasped Zen better than the scholar Shen-hsiu. A Vedantist with whom I studied, a man of great moral integrity and intellectual power, when I delicately inquired about his own spiritual progress, answered that he could not attain moksha because of his incorrigible tendency to think. If thinking and intellect are not required for attaining the Absolute, what is? There is no one answer to this question. There are three answers. One answer is the capacity to purge experience of all separateness between the conscious mind and the object of which it is conscious. Psychologically this might be interpreted as regression to a primitive state of mind in which the distinction of subject and object has not yet been made, and so being literally like a little, a very little, child. A second answer is the capacity to free experience of all objectivity. Psychologically this might be interpreted as pure assertion of the libido or will apart from those objects to which it is normally directed because it cares for them. A third answer is the capacity to free experience of all subjectivity. Psychologically this might be interpreted as psychic honesty, reflecting the given as it is rather than as one wishes, consciously or unconsciously, that it be. These three capacities for freeing feeling, willing, and knowing from one another are incompatible, and the goals of Love, Freedom, and Truth to which they lead are alternatives which cannot coexist in the same individual. Commitment and coexistence imply each other. Commitment is in the individual. Coexistence is in the society.

The question still arises whether any intuitive meaning,

as contrasted with definition by extrapolation, can be given to the notion of absolute experience. Persons progressing along any of the three paths may have experiences which are partial or imperfect copies of the absolute experience, but ordinary non-religious experience might seem to offer nothing to show the quality of the Absolute. The absolute experience in any of its alternative forms is eternal and ineffable. This, to be sure, is to be expected. As Kant taught, time, which is the form of the phenomenal world, both physical and mental, because it is our form of intuition, is in us, not we in it, and our categories of understanding are also relevant to the phenomenal world, not to the Absolute. Nevertheless, there are normal, commonplace, and often daily experiences of ordinary men which are like the Absolute in quality and so in a way intimate what the Absolute may be. Mystical writers in the Christian, Sufi, and Vaishnava traditions regularly use sexual love as an analogue of religious love, and the more outspoken writers make the sexual climax an analogue of absolute Love. This is, of course, a mere figure of speech, but they use it because they consider it an appropriate figure. Absolute Love is infinite and eternal, and the other Person is God, yet the quality of the experience is somehow the same. Zen Buddhists emphasize the significance of the tea ceremony, concerning which Suzuki says:

> To take a cup of tea with friends in this environment, talking probably about the Sumiye sketch in the alcove or some art topic suggested by the tea-utensils in the room, wonderfully lifts the mind above the perplexities of life. The warrior is saved from his daily occupation of fighting and the businessman from his ever-present idea of money-making. Is it not something, indeed, to find in this world of struggles and vanities a corner, however humble, where one can rise above the limits of relativity and even have a glimpse of eternity?[4]

4. D. T. Suzuki, *Zen Buddhism* (Garden City: Doubleday, 1956), 294.

The ritual and utensils are not essential; one may sit on a chair and use an American cup. What is essential is the detachment and freedom from distraction which gives this simple activity, pure activity without desire or purpose and therefore incapable of being thwarted, hackneyed and trivial as it is in itself, the quality of nirvana. Vedanta philosophers distinguish three states of ordinary consciousness—waking, dreaming, and deep dreamless sleep—and say that deep sleep is a foretaste of moksha, eternal freedom from illusion, and mukti, eternal bliss. We remember deep sleep after waking, so consciousness persisted, although without illusory objects, and we remember it as blissful, the happiest kind of sleep. These common experiences are alike in being quasi-ineffable: they cannot be described in terms of anything else or known except by personal experience. They are alike in being quasi-eternal: time seems to stop for the moment. But they are radically different from each other in quality—the first physical and spiritual union, the second detached action, the third pure passivity. In the first separateness, in the second influence of environment, in the third mind's creative activity ceases, though only for a moment. All are blissful, in their diverse, alternative, and incompatible ways. They are intimations of the Absolute in ordinary life.

Be this as it may, a tenable theory of religion is possible only by clear thinking, which analyses experience, indicates the Absolute, and exorcises the demon of monism. What is important, however, is not the theory of religion, based on alternative forms of the Absolute, but the practice of religion, based on commitment and coexistence. This is only a dream. It is a dream which has been fulfilled in other aspects of life, aspects in which our civilization has attained some degree of success. In academic life, it is fulfilled by the departmentalization of the university. It seems obvious to me that the Philosophy Department is the most important one, but I would be surprised and dismayed if all my colleagues thought so. In social organization, it is fulfilled by the division of labour which makes civilization possible. My vocation is teaching and re-search, but I do not despise my neighbours with other vocations, nor do I pretend that what they do is really a sort of teaching and research. In domestic relations, it is fulfilled by monogamy. I do not say that my wife is the most beautiful woman in the world and I will fight any man who denies it; I do not say that I suppose, after all, she is no more beautiful than the others; I say she is the most beautiful woman in the world but do not expect you to say so. But the dream has not been fulfilled in the two most important aspects of life, politics, which maintains peace, and religion, which seeks ultimate values, aspects in which our civilization is conspicuously unsuccessful, unsuccessful just because either dogmatic violence or lib-eral non-commitment, not coexistence of alternatives, has been the rule. We all have a dream, a dream revived after each world war, not of nations fighting each other and not of a world state with homogeneous culture but of many diverse nations each sovereign and demanding its own citizens' loyalty but coexisting in a League of Nations or United Nations. I also have a dream of religions neither opposing each other nor abandoning their commitment to the Absolute, each to its own form of the Absolute, coex-isting in their coordinate but radically different aspirations. Then will be fulfilled the word of the Prophet: "For all people will walk every one in the name of *his* god, and we will walk in the name of the Lord *our* God for ever and ever."